Education:
An Introduction

Education:
An Introduction

HAROLD LOUKES, JOHN WILSON
and BARBARA COWELL

Martin Robertson · Oxford

© John Wilson, 1983

First published in 1983 by
Martin Robertson & Company Ltd.,
108 Cowley Road, Oxford OX4 1JF.

British Library Cataloguing in Publication Data

Loukes, Harold
  Education.
  1. Education
  I. Title   II. Wilson, John
  III. Cowell, Barbara
  370   LB17
  ISBN 0-85520-598-9
  ISBN 0-85520-599-7 Pbk

Typeset in 10 on 12pt English by Pioneer, East Sussex
Printed and bound in Great Britain by
Billings, Worcester

Contents

Preface

This book is intended as an introduction to the study of education, designed primarily for teachers and student-teachers. It is a joint product, the result of work done by the late Harold Loukes, who was recently Reader in Education at Oxford University, and by us. In a note that follows, one of us will try to say something about Harold's contribution and about how the book is put together: here we confine ourselves to its general plan and purpose.

We take the view — widely held in many circles, but not often voiced and certainly unfashionable — that the successful study and practice of education depend chiefly upon clarity, common sense and freedom from various kinds of prejudice, and that these qualities are more important for the practising teacher than a wide and profound knowledge either of educational theory or of contemporary educational practice and fashionable educational ideals. Both of these latter are much publicized, but there is comparatively little literature that aims, as this book aims, at increasing the reader's own ability to see his way through educational problems. This is not an easy task; indeed, it is perhaps partly because it is so challenging that people have been tempted to abandon it in favour of other approaches — to stress the latest theoretical ideas or topics currently thought to be most 'relevant' or 'practical'. Whatever may be the value of such approaches, there is certainly plenty of literature based on them, and we do not aim to add to it here.

The first part of the book enlarges on these points; in this we attempt to give some general account of what is involved in being a teacher, what the enterprise of education is primarily about and what the serious study of education involves (chapters 1—3). In Part II (chapters 4—10) we deal with a number of topics, all of which we take to be central to the teacher's or educator's interests, and all of which are cases in which (we believe) a lot of contemporary thinking has gone badly astray. We hope in this way not only to shed some light on the topics but also to show the reader how important it is to think for oneself and not simply to echo current fashions. Naturally, there is a great deal more to be said about each topic than space allows us to say here; but it is the way in which people *begin* to think about the topics that we take to be peculiarly important. In education, as in much else, when things go wrong they usually go wrong right at the start. Making the right initial approach is more than half the battle.

The literature on these topics is enormous; but rather than clutter up the text with footnotes and offer the reader an immense bibliography, we have given only a short reading list at the end of the book. Items on this list include those works that (in our judgement) adopt the same kind of common-sense, clear and non-technical approach as we are trying to adopt in this book.

J.B.W.
B.C.
Oxford, 1982.

Note and Acknowledgements

This note is in no sense a general account of Harold Loukes' life and work; but I owe it to the reader (as well as to Harold's memory) to make plain how this book arose and how it is put together. What I say may also help to explain its general thrust and purpose.

I do not venture any claim to have been among those closest to Harold as a person; but I can, perhaps, claim to have shared many of his thoughts on education as intimately, and in as much detail, as most of his other colleagues. 'Shared' in two senses: first, in that by attending his lectures and seminars, as well as by taking part in more informal conversation, I was able to understand how he thought on most important educational topics; secondly, in that my own thoughts turned out to be remarkably similar, indeed often almost identical (in part, certainly, because they were influenced by his own).

In his lifetime he published comparatively little on general educational topics; most of his best-known work deals with religious and moral education and with the education of teenagers. That he held strong and well-considered views on other topics was, of course, clear to those who knew him, however, and is confirmed by unpublished writing that survives him. This consists of, first, some fairly continuous manuscript, dealing centrally with the professionalism of teachers and the nature of education. Much of this material arose from the very well-attended seminars that he gave under the title of 'The Pedocratic Oath' ('pedocratic' being construed — by riding roughshod over the original Greek, as he well knew — by analogy with 'Hippocratic'), an attempt to determine what teachers could reasonably bind themselves to as professionals (see chapter 1). His unpublished work also included a large quantity of more or less fragmentary notes and jottings. Some of this book consists of the first, with emendations by myself and Barbara Cowell (on grounds of style rather than content: the manuscript was not in its final form), but most of it is based on the second, filled out by my memory of conversations with him and cross-checked by inquiries made of students who attended his seminars. Clearly, the general style and presentation of the book must be our responsibility; but there is (we feel confident) at least nothing there with which Harold would have strongly disagreed.

Harold stood firmly for what one might call the human or humane tradition in education, a tradition perhaps best defined by reference to its enemies. Like most (I am tempted to say, all) serious thinkers on the subject, he regarded education as essentially an interpersonal transaction, involving a kind of personal relationship and initiation into some distinctively human form of thought or shared experience. This tradition has, of course, a good many advocates even in these days: one thinks of Bantock, Peters, Hirst and plenty of others. But it is threatened from one quarter by the still essentially scientific, if now more sharply criticized, methodology of the social sciences, which — even, I think, in their more humane guises — have so far failed to come to terms with the tiresome fact that people are radically unlike planets or even rats; from another quarter by the increased emphasis on 'practical skills' (a phrase about which he was particularly scathing) that has arisen from a (very proper) disenchantment with educational theory; from a third by bureaucratic, political and administrative pressures, important elements in themselves but ones that (particularly in times of recession or social change) are always liable to invade the conceptual and practical space properly occupied by considerations more directly to do with truth and human beings; and from a fourth by the neo-romanticism of those who, not content that the heart's affections should be holy, have taken them as the only important criterion of what ought to be done in education (here too Harold, with the additional expertise of a scholar in English literature, was often at his most debunking).

Some of these threats to the human(e) tradition became stronger, or at least more visible, during the last part of his career: in particular what he saw as a busy, pseudo-practical and managerial professionalism which has little time for the intelligent and non-political amateur. 'Professionalism' and 'amateur' should be in quotes here, since he held that the kind of professionalism displayed by social scientists, educational impresarios and the chairmen of most educational committees is not, in fact, appropriate to education at all, and that the intelligent and perceptive amateur does much better. Harold recognized, naturally, that certain areas of human life are peculiarly liable to corruption, fantasy, prejudice and psychological compulsion, that education is one of these areas and that any serious person working in such a field must inevitably feel alienated from much of what goes on. But towards the end of his life, which came very soon after his retirement, various reasons combined to prevent him from rising above that (admittedly depressing) recognition with the buoyancy and ebullience of earlier years. Invariably helpful to those who sought his aid, and always willing to converse when conversation appeared profitable, he nevertheless came to disengage himself rather more sharply from some of the contemporary disputes; sometimes, like one of Jane Austen's heroines, refusing the more obviously stupid or prejudiced 'the compliment of rational disagreement'. It may be that increased disenchantment with the movements of educational fashion and the (often invincible) ignorance of some of its leaders made him disinclined to put his notes and thoughts into publishable shape as rapidly as he might have done. But there is little doubt that many people will want to know what he thought about these matters; and I am glad to repair what might otherwise have been a serious loss to the educational world.

Harold's genius lay in his intuitive grasp of what was sane, sensible and imaginative, particularly in reference to people and learning. He was able not only to think well but also — like Socrates and other outstanding educators — to communicate and relate well to people: and that is putting it mildly, as generations of students and colleagues will testify. This is, I take it, the kind of genius peculiarly relevant to education; but the propositions and beliefs that flow from it do not lend themselves immediately to proof by argument from one or the other of any well established intellectual disciplines. Many of our conversations involved an attempt on my part to see how his insights could be verified (or falsified) by more careful and stringent philosophical analysis; and

I think we made a good deal of progress, which is (I hope) represented by the more specifically philosophical approach of some of the chapters in this book. But although he was well read in philosophy and understood the point of conceptual analysis, his own bent did not lie there; it lay somewhere between the expertise of the literary critic and that of the psychotherapist — as this description suggests, extremely difficult even to define, much more to justify by generalized argument. If any of this is to be imparted to the reader, it will come through only piecemeal and in detail.

I ought in justice to add that there were significant differences between us: not, curiously, in the actual content of what we might say about educational topics, but in the psychological tone, or style, or perhaps background to this content. Even to try to state these is to run a big risk, but it might not too misleadingly be said that Harold was less optimistic, brisk, cheerful and (one might say) unrealistic and dictatorial than I. He entertained more sombre and Hardyesque feelings about the human condition, possibly stemming from an extremely severe childhood: I myself, brought up in a more liberal and intellectual tradition, have always to resist the feeling that even the most unreasonable people can be set right by one or two quick tutorials. I mention this only in order to say that, if something of this brisk or dictatorial optimism of style emerges, that is my fault and not his.

Finally, some thanks and acknowledgements. First, the task of putting this book together, in the rather complicated way described above, involved far more work than I could have undertaken alone. Though I was happy (as being more familiar with Harold's thought) to take charge of its general plan and content, a great deal of that work was done by Barbara Cowell, who is in every sense my co-author. Her agreement with my own and Harold's views allows us to use the word 'we' throughout the book, since we are bold enough to believe that all three of us may fairly be represented as speaking with a single voice. Secondly, there has been inevitably some overlap and repetition of what one or other of us has said or written elsewhere. This is unavoidable (and not, in my judgement, regrettable) for general or (in a broad sense) philosophical writers like ourselves, who have often to make the same essential points in different contexts. To track down every case of this would be difficult or impossible; but we should like here to acknowledge some repetition from the following works mentioned in the bibliography: Loukes 1959 and 1973, Wilson 1975, 1979a and 1979b; from my essay in *The Ethical Dimensions of the School Curriculum* (ed. Lionel Ward), published in 1982 by the University College of Swansea, Faculty of Education; and from articles in the *British Journal of Educational Studies* and *Westminster Studies in Education*. I apologize in advance to those concerned if I have failed to mention any other significant overlaps. Last and most important, I must express my thanks to Mary Loukes for making Harold's manuscript and notes available, and for trusting me to use them in this way. I can only hope the result justifies that trust, and that fellow-workers in the enterprise of education will find the book helpful.

J.B.W.
Oxford, 1982

Part I

1

The Teacher's Commitments

What is it like to be a teacher today? In particular, is it necessary for a teacher to be good — *really* good, that is to say, especially and particularly good, good in the way Samuel Butler said clergymen had to be ('the clergyman is expected to be a kind of human Sunday') in *The Way of All Flesh?*

Not long ago these would have been absurd or unnecessary questions. Teachers, their pupils and their pupils' parents, institutions such as the Church and the press, and indeed all decent people anywhere, shared a fairly clear consensus about what a teacher was supposed to be like and how he was supposed to behave. He — and, of course, even more she — were respectable, wearing respectable clothes, living in respectable houses, usually at a respectable distance from the school. They would not be heard to swear, or drink too much, or hold hands (even if they were engaged to be married) within the neighbourhood of the school; there were unwritten rules forbidding such things. Inside school there was a similar, even more rigorous set of rules: a clear distance between teacher and pupil, which neither side would attempt to cross except with calculated offensiveness, easily recognized on the one side as cheek and on the other as sarcasm; a certain gravity, not incompatible with a vast amount of rather conventional humour but excluding a shared giggle; a distance not merely in personal living space but in intellectual status as well — the teacher knew it all, and he could not be wrong.

This picture is over-simple, of course. There were individuals who broke the respectable image, some with permission (art

3

masters and the like), some without permission; becoming, in the process, 'characters'. Some schools deliberately set out to destroy the stereotype, often rather sadly and earnestly ('We go about in the nude a lot here,' said the headmaster of one famous progressive school). There were social class differences: the 'schoolmaster' was subtly different from the 'teacher', while the 'schoolmistress' hovered between the two. The young schoolmaster shrank from the mask, trusting in his own winning ways; the older one preferred a mask specially made by himself, but found it increasingly comfortable to wear.

The public language about it all was very pompous. Consider what Cyril Norwood wrote in 1929 in *The English Tradition of Education*. Education, he was arguing, was a noble cause, the effort to produce leaders in a war between light and darkness:

> It seems a far cry to return to the remote and dimly-seen figure of the great Alfred, but it is not too far to recognize in outline the true vision which sees in education that single system which prepares citizens to serve a united nation. Alfred's task was to lead an illiterate people against an alien race of invaders . . . and . . . he saw that his folk needed most of all leaders . . . The light which Alfred kindled was never entirely put out . . . (p. 9)

It shone first, he tells us, in the schools of chivalry, in:

> the apprenticeship to riding and the use of arms, to hunting and open-air sport, to the tilt-yard and the realities of warfare, but behind all this . . . was a great moral ideal of conduct. 'To ride abroad, redressing human wrongs', to serve one lady in all purity and fidelity, these were noble ideals. (pp. 9—10)

This heady language continues through the whole story of the unity of the single nation, sadly jarred by Reformation and Renaissance but bound together again by Arnold and Thring and Almond, Sanderson, Vaughan and Temple and other great educators of the Victorian and Edwardian ages:

> For what has happened in the course of the last hundred years is that the old ideals have been recaptured. The old ideal of chivalry which inspired the knighthood of medieval days, the ideal of training for the service of the community, which inspired the greatest of the men who founded schools for their own day and for posterity, have been combined in the tradition of English education which holds the field today. It is based upon religion:

it relies largely upon games and effort: it has developed an intellectual appeal on many sides . . . it has cast its Puritanism, and has no longer any fear of art, or music, or even the drama. It is inspired by the duty of preparing all for the service of their generation. (p. 20)

And so, finally:

There are three positions which in the face of this insidious and non-moral power [i.e. the unacceptable face of capitalism] must at all costs be defended. They are the supremacy of mind, the tradition of culture, and the institution of the family. And once again I return to my text, and declare that these can alone be safeguarded by a teaching profession which is united by a single ideal, and has the power to base the education which it imparts on religion, discipline, culture, and service. (p. 316)

Whatever way we think of this, the important thing is that it is not just Norwood speaking: it is the general voice. These words would have gone down well in the keynote speech, on a Friday evening, at a weekend conference on 'Education: Whence and Whither?' Today, we do not need to say, it has all changed or is at least changing. We believe not that the contemporary teacher has any less concern or is less caring, though he might not want to use this kind of language, but that we have lost the consensus about what the teacher is like and what he does. Consider this extract from *The First Year of Teaching* (Hannan *et al.,* 1976). (It is written by a man.)

Teaching a class of sevens, eights, and nines makes me realize how much my position is a caring one. It is unnerving to realize how much trust the children do have in one almost automatically. It is easy to feel too motherly and protective . . . Perhaps these days men are less afraid of feeling motherly. I certainly do not feel it an insult to my virility if I realize I have been motherly . . . though I suppose I do tend to take a paternal role more often than a maternal one. Another thing I have noticed to my surprise is that women in school seem to find it harder to relax into the motherly role than the men. Certainly no one could have felt less confident that I in those first few weeks when to my surprise the children did do what they were told, they did stay quiet when I asked them to. I gazed incredulously on my brood patiently awaiting my instructions. (p. 107)

Norwood's generation would have found this incomprehensible. 'Caring', they would have said, 'all right, but what is all this about motherly roles and paternal roles? If you must use barbarous words like "role", at least talk of a *teacher's* role, and have done with it. School is no place for playing mothers and fathers: just be a teacher. And as for being incredulous when your brood awaits your instructions, isn't that what they are there for?' But nowadays the brood does not always await instructions or believe in the teacher's role. Consider this, from a secondary school:

> Sometimes they'd sit in the front row — the troublemakers often used to come to the front not the back — and just to make life difficult they'd have a farting contest or something. The whole room would suddenly start to stink so I'd go round and open a window and I'd say, 'The next bloke who farts just goes outside.'

Or this from a primary school:

> It happened to me very often with the junior boys, nine-, ten-, eleven-year-olds — as you walked past they would grab at you. It was nothing on duty in the playground getting a couple of hands up your skirt . . . When I was first on duty in the playground I remember boys lying down on their stomachs at my feet. For ages I didn't understand why, I didn't know whether it was hero-worship or not — there were boys everywhere at my feet. I suddenly realized they were looking up my skirt. I had a mother in the last term to say that her daughter was very upset, she'd been awake during the night, because the boys in my class were putting their hands up her skirt. And I immediately thought, well, I can't say, yes, I promise it will stop, when it happens to me, so I said, 'Yes, it does happen, but I'll do my best.' And I didn't feel I could announce it to the class and say, 'Please, boys, don't put your hands up the skirts' because it would go on all the more. (p. 85)

There are problems here other than the one we are considering, but at least it is clear that the settled and effective stereotype of 'teacher' or 'sir' or 'miss' is not what it was.

Now, stereotypes are supposed to be bad, and we are all supposed to rejoice when they are broken. But even today, when we have work to do it is helpful if certain expectations can be understood both by the worker and by those among whom he works. The task is made easier if we can turn to it without having too many other matters to deal with, too many other problems on our mind. Equally, the task is better performed if everybody understands not merely the task itself but the manner in which it will be performed, and if the personal style appropriate to it is agreed.

But behind all this lies a harder question, the question with which we began. Must teachers be *good*? The Norwood answer would have been, 'Yes, of course. They must be *better* than ordinary people, because they are models, inspirers, a reference point for the rest of their pupils' lives.' And so, the distancing, the self-control, the presentation of learning and virtue were accepted without question as part of the schoolmaster's life. But is this view correct? And do we believe it now?

The question may be put into focus by expressing it in the form, 'Should teachers have a Hippocratic Oath of their own?' This oath was inherited from the Hippocratic Books in ancient Greece and regarded as a statement of the general nature of the commitment of the doctor. It is not at all certain that anyone actually swore the oath, or to whom he would have sworn it if he did, but the gist of it still represents something that is a working reality in the profession, the 'professing', the promising, of the medical practitioner. It runs like this:

I will look upon him who shall have taught me this art even as one of my parents. I will share my substance with him, and I will supply his necessities, if he be in need. I will regard his offspring even as my own brethren, and I will teach them this Art, if they would learn it, without fee or covenant. I will impart this Art by precept, by lecture and by every mode of teaching, not only to my own sons but to the sons of him who has taught me, and to disciples bound by covenant and oath, according to the law of Medicine.

The regimen I shall adopt shall be for the benefit of my patients according to my ability and judgement, and not for their hurt or for any wrong. I will give no deadly drug to any, though it will be asked of me, nor will I counsel such and especially I will not aid a woman to procure an abortion.

Whatever house I enter, there will I go for the benefit of the sick, refraining from all wrongdoing or corruption, and especially from any act of seduction, of male and female, of bond or free. Whatsoever things I see or hear concerning the life of men, in my attendance on the sick or even apart therefrom which ought not to be noised abroad, I will keep silence thereon, counting such things as sacred secrets.

Leaving aside the circumstances of the time, such as the lack of old-age pensions or free education, and modern disagreements over abortion and similar problems, there are three general levels or categories of commitment here. First, there is the actuality of the medical profession and its task, the people who practise it and those who may practise it; a commitment to the survival of honest medicine, not the private power of one man but the availability and perpetuation of the tradition of medical knowledge and service. Second, there are the objectives of the art of healing, the health and life of the patients. And, finally, there is the refusal to take advantage of the peculiar opportunities put in the hands of the practitioner by the practice of his art, arising from the intimacy of the task through physical contact and the accidental knowledge of the private lives of his patients.

(1) By his commitment to the profession, in the first paragraph, the new doctor accepts responsibility for the openness and integrity of the healing art. 'I will *impart* this art,' he says. 'I will not hug my knowledge or my discoveries to myself; I will seek to pass on what I know, to make my successful practices accessible to anyone who shares my commitment to healing. And I will be loyal to other teachers and healers: I will honour those who taught me and will sustain and care for initiates; I promise my strength to defend the strength of medical men everywhere.' We are not discussing medical ethics, but the point here is that the reception of medical knowledge by the student brings with it the obligation to pass such knowledge on; and the first moral move he makes is a move of loyalty, of humility if you like, of denying his own desires. 'When I join this brotherhood,' the student says, 'I cease, in a measure, to be my own man.'

(2) The commitment to the objectives of medicine also raises controversial matters, and the contemporary medical scene is littered with moral problems. But again the point is worth making, since it is still powerfully at work in medical practice: medicine is about healing and not about power, or scientific research, or demonstrating skill, or social engineering.

(3) The recognition of the doctor's peculiar opportunities, the side-effects of his work without which he cannot do his work, is still pertinent enough; and the open declaration that he would

regard any abuse of his power as wrong is still important. It is agreed that a doctor who seduces a patient, all things being equal, does worse than an ordinary seducer who has no unfair advantage. A doctor still knows a great deal about his patients that they would prefer to keep from anybody else. Neither of these accidental powers, the oath declares, must be indulged.

We pay this much attention to the Hippocratic Oath simply to raise the question: could there be, for the teacher, a corresponding 'Pedocratic Oath' in which his moral commitment is articulated? And if there were, what would it contain? We must make clear at this point that we are not contemplating a formal oath to be sworn by young teachers, as soldiers, or magistrates, or witnesses in the box swear oaths. It is not clear that these oaths prompt any actual change in behaviour: fearsomely sworn though they may be, some soldiers turn out to be less than faithful to the authorities; some witnesses lie as happily on oath as off it. And the young teacher may not be made more loyal by reciting the oath, even in Latin. We view the oath as a kind of map of the territory into which one enters after promising to teach: 'I promise to teach, and therefore I promise to behave in a certain way.' The first part of this undertaking is obvious ('I promise to teach, and therefore I shall teach'), but there is something more — more personal, more moral — that we propose to explore. The territory lies somewhere between that of a commitment that is 'true for all times and places', which is an acutely difficult proposition in the context of morality, and that of 'specific rules laid down for particular people by a local club', which is tolerably simple. Let us look again at the medical profession. There are certain rules laid down by the British Medical Association or the hospital doctors that apply firmly enough in specific situations but could not be justified as moral principles even for doctors. But there are some moral principles that are the necessary conditions of the successful pursuit of medicine, with constant applicability. Thus it is not 'in the nature of things' that healing could not be accomplished without medical solidarity or without agreed rules against seduction or blackmail. Without these rules medicine could, in principle, be carried on, but in practice it would not be carried on for long. The rules are not in the nature of *things,* but they are in the nature of *people.* A doctor who cured the master but seduced the mistress before he left would soon lose his clients. The behaviour of people is as obstinate, or nearly as obstinate, a moral fact as the behaviour of the body after absorbing poison.

Then what would a 'Pedocratic Oath' look like? We have seen that the Hippocratic Oath outlines three areas of commitment: to the medical profession, to the objectives of medicine and to the refusal to exploit, for private gain, the peculiar opportunities and temptations thrown in a doctor's way. Is this a helpful structure for the moral commitment of teachers?

(1) Commitment to the Profession

The first act that the teacher performs is to join an already existing group of people who are maintaining the enterprise of education. It is not impossible to imagine acts of teaching performed outside formal education: the de-schoolers claim to imagine such acts, and the medieval universities followed after teaching rather than originating it (though it could be argued, of course, that in the medieval university teachers were already workers in an ecclesiastical industry of which education was one department). But though it is imaginable that people with something to teach might simply set themselves up and teach, with no commitment to the profession and a simple commitment to their entirely voluntary pupils, the fact is that teachers do join the profession and, having joined it, they accept some measure of commitment to it. The teacher acknowledges the right of the profession to judge his merits, though he may not think it does him justice, and he implicitly promises, in some way and in some degree, to behave as the profession believes a teacher should.

Even this cautious statement of obligation is perhaps not self-evident. Suppose a highly intellectual angel were sent on a special mission to infiltrate the profession and to demonstrate from within what a teacher would be like if he were uncorrupted by society. He would still have to submit himself to the usual tests of fitness, appear in an examination room and write the correct things, and appear for some weeks in a classroom and cause some children to learn. This he might of course, do, in an entirely cynical spirit, promising himself freedom of action when all this was over. (Many human candidates for the profession do this.) But when somebody finally hands him a group of children, the 'somebody' (headmaster, governors, local councillors acting on behalf of parents) implicitly makes certain demands. The now qualified angel is not free to do something totally other than 'educate', though he is given some freedom in deciding what 'education' means; he cannot remove the children's appendixes or teach them whatever he likes. He will have to accept, broadly, the teacher's conventional role. This cannot be pressed to the point where he hands himself over to the powers of darkness, but in accepting these children he accepts them on terms that have already been laid down.

In a similar spirit, the teacher promises, by joining at all, to obey (to some degree) those already occupying posts of command, however unsatisfactory he may find them. Education, even informal education, is a venture that calls for prior organization and requires new teachers to fall in with what is going on. It is not a venture that happens just because some inspired people step forward to do it. Warnock (1971), arguing that 'generalized beneficence' is not enough for the effective improvement of the human situation, writes:

> The following analogy may be of some help here. Suppose that to confront an enemy on the field of battle, I assemble, say, fifty thousand men, all fired with the single overriding aim of victory. What will be the best way of securing this end? It does not seem — in this case — at all paradoxical to say that the end will *not* be most effectively pursued by telling each man so to act as, in his judgement, best to achieve it; even if all my men are highly sagacious and experienced soldiers, mere chaos will ensue, since the task thus set them is not merely difficult but completely impossible. Clearly enough, none can act effectively entirely on his own; but equally clearly, none can tell what his part should best be in any corporate enterprise unless he knows how others are going to act — and how can he know that, since each is faced with just the same hopeless uncertainty as he is himself? Even if my army should manage to get itself on parade — and it is not really clear how it would manage to do even that — any ensuing action, however splendidly intentioned on the part of each, would be a mere welter of conflicting, unco-ordinated, self-defeating, unvictorious confusion.

Similarly, the educational army could not get itself into classrooms at the same time as a group of children without help from some kind of authority, nor teach what the children should learn on Tuesday unless someone had taught what they needed before

Tuesday, nor — but we need not go on. How far the young teacher needs to go in obedience is another matter; but that the first teaching act is an act of obedience, of self-abnegation, is unarguable.

(2) Commitment to Education

The second area of commitment is to the nature and objectives of education itself. At one level this statement is trite. But it is by no means clear what 'education' is; and it is certain that anyone engaging in it *without* getting clear what it is will operate at second-hand, under the unexamined influence of the tradition, those in authority, or the random consequences of his own whims. Teachers are in greater difficulty here than are doctors, who have a much broader base of agreement about what 'health' is than teachers have about what being educated is, what education is for, who ought to have it, who ought to decide these questions, whether it is in the end for society or for the individual who is being educated (and if for the individual, whether it is for his happiness, or well-being, or efficiency in the future, or for his happiness now or, indeed, for his happiness at all rather than for some kind of increase in awareness that, in an unhappy world, can only increase his unhappiness).

These questions, put with sufficient cunning, could throw any conference on education into disarray. They are, for the most part, hard to answer in a form clear and determined enough to provide practical guidance. And even if we were to succeed in answering a few, we should not know what to do next because we do not know how to guarantee the securing of such objectives. How does anybody, for example, *make* a child happy now? We can stop him crying in various ways, but can we *make* him happy? And if it is difficult to be sure of that now, how can we say we could achieve it for him at, say, the age of 35? And would it last until he was 45? How, for example, ought we to conduct sex education so as to guarantee every boy and girl a happy sex life? And should that be 'now' or 'then'?

The practical man would shrug these questions off. But anyone who educates starts to interfere with another person's life in such a way that consequences for the victim's happiness, and his usefulness, are inevitable. There is thus a moral responsibility to

conduct some sort of examination of the issues and of the possible
consequences of the business of teaching, just as someone who
cannot drive is responsible for considering the consequences of
releasing the brakes of a car at the top of a hill. Walking in a
minefield is never a safe occupation, but at least one walks
differently for knowing it *is* a minefield.

(3) The Rejection of Exploitation

Finally, there is an area of commitment concerned with the
opportunities of exercising power that arise inevitably in teaching.
The teacher has the power to lead his pupils and must therefore
have the power to mislead them. He is given the status of one who
knows more than his pupils, and therefore has a kind of academic
authority that has its dangers. Nobody would nowadays have the
uncritical respect that was accorded to Goldsmith's schoolmaster,
'when still the wonder grew/That one small head could carry all he
knew'; but still the teacher is trusted to know what he is teaching,
and he is not easily found out. Pupils are skilled at penetrating
personal insincerity, but not as well equipped to spot academic
errors. Nor can they easily detect bias. Bias is part of what they
learn, and until they later encounter another bias, they are easy
victims of indoctrination.

Also included among the teacher's special opportunities and
temptations is the necessity for close and continuous personal
relations within which teaching is performed. It is possible to
imagine teaching taking place in a cool, clinical atmosphere, but in
practice classrooms full of children are emotional places, full of
love and hate and affection and delight and anger and dismay.
Children learn better from somebody they like, and a warm
interplay of feeling keeps minds awake and alive. But there can be
problems with this. How warm is productively warm? Where, in
these likings and dislikings, does favouritism begin? (It is no good
pretending that teachers do, or can, like all children equally. If
they did, they would simply have no taste. They can only try to
treat them all equally.) And what, precisely, is wrong with
favouritism? And is it healthy for the generalized affectionate tone
of the classroom to spark off friendships *outside* the school? And if
friendships, then what about love affairs? And what is to be said
about punishment? The teacher has a duty to maintain such order

as is necessary to learning and must be allowed sanctions of some sort. But what sort? And how much of what sort? Anybody who examines the concept of punishment comes out, in the end, in its defence: but establishing the right to punish does not carry with it the right to send a boy to Siberia for spelling 'accommodation' with one m. And even if a teacher is fair and rational, how does he weigh the needs of the class against the needs of a particular pupil, the needs of learning here and now against the needs of growing up with a modicum of self-confidence, the needs of the class against the demands of his own personal threshold ('Look, I know it's terribly unfair, but unless you shut up now, *this minute,* I shall go mad')?

The commitment to avoid abuses must also include, as it does for the doctor, a promise of discretion. Teachers acquire a great deal of knowledge about their pupils and about their pupils' parents and home conditions ('Please, Miss, *my* Mum says . . .', 'My favourite relative is . . .'). And the record cards are filled with big-brotherish information, institutionalized indiscretions. Staff who have to handle difficult children need access to this information. Courts ask for information. Potential employers ask for information. Sometimes a pupil's classmates need to be let a little into the secret of somebody's misbehaviour ('Her mother died on Tuesday', 'Her parents were divorced on Tuesday', 'Her father beat her mother up on Tuesday, and she had to go to hospital'). How far does one go?

———————

Of the three parts of this 'Pedocratic Oath', it should be clear that we must regard the second — the commitment to education — as centrally important. There are two main reasons for this.

First, there is a sense in which the other two commitments depend upon it. It is to the *teaching* profession that the intending teacher commits himself, not just to any profession, and he is bound only to the extent that the profession does its proper job. If, for instance, the teaching profession were to be controlled by Nazis who were interested only in indoctrinating people and being cruel to Jews, the sensible teacher could no longer feel obliged to be loyal to it. Furthermore, what counts as the 'exploitation' or 'abuse' of privacy and personal relationships will probably depend on whether this or that type of behaviour is *educative*. The teacher's commitment to education prevents him from taking unfair advantage of his pupils; the way in which he uses private knowledge or intimacy has to be governed by the question 'Will this help the child's education or not?'

Secondly, teachers are inevitably involved in the enterprise of education. They do not only teach; they also engage (like it or not) in pastoral care, informal relationships with pupils, planning curricula, adopting some sort of attitude to new subjects like moral education, dealing with parents, relating to local educational authorities and many other things. Indeed, if 'teaching' is taken to be equivalent to 'instructing', only a very small part of a teacher's time is thus taken up, and that part might perhaps often be done as well or better by a teaching machine, or a book, or a television lecture. The teacher is necessary not because we need instruction machines but because he *educates*; and only people can educate people. We must turn, then, to a discussion of what education is.

2

Education and its Enemies

We start with some simple propositions:

1 There are a number of human enterprises, distinguishable from each other, that we classify under such headings as 'medicine', 'art', 'education', 'science' and so on.
2 These enterprises characteristically have different purposes and aim at different kinds of goods: because of this their methods of procedure, governing rules and criteria for success are different.
3 In order to be practised successfully, or at all, each enterprise needs certain necessary conditions to be fulfilled ('necessary', because there is a logical connection between the conditions and the enterprise).
4 It is always possible, and very often happens, that an enterprise is neglected, misunderstood, eroded, obliterated, overridden or in some way damaged or corrupted by particular circumstances.

We keep these propositions simple and general because we want to avoid complex questions about what is to count as the proper way of distinguishing between one enterprise and another, what particular verbal markers (the titles of each enterprise) normally mean in various languages, what are the nature and details of the necessary conditions, and any other sophisticated problems that might be thought relevant. We will just say that if someone were to maintain, for instance, that there is *no* way of satisfactorily distinguishing between 'medicine' and 'art', that medicine does not aim at goods (e.g. health) different from those that art aims at, that there are no necessary requirements for the successful practice of medicine (even the ability to inspect a patient's body and to treat it physically) or that certain circumstances might not make it difficult or impossible for medicine to flourish, we do not want to argue with him here.

Ought we to start, then, by 'defining' education? Something turns here on what is to count as 'defining'. Many people nowadays are reluctant, perhaps with some justice, to talk about the 'definition', of the 'essence', of education; and it is true that a very great deal has been written under headings like 'The aims of education', 'The nature of education', 'The concept of education' and so forth, most of which is more confusing than helpful. It is better to start by asking ourselves what it is that such discussions are attempting to clarify, why we *need* to consider the 'concept' or the 'nature' of education. Suppose we are teachers, or educational administrators, or researchers, or civil servants in some Ministry of Education: what is the point of engaging in reflection about education?

To this question the answer is reasonably clear, we think. It is, quite simply, so that we can have an adequate and consciously held view about what we are trying to do, about the nature of the enterprise in which we are engaging. Now, of course, actual people in actual jobs — teachers, civil servants and so on — will be engaged from time to time in many different enterprises. A teacher does not only teach: he may also keep the register, referee football matches, attend union meetings and so on — and in time of war or some other crisis he may find himself having to keep his pupils safe from bombs or plague. Similarly, a doctor does not only cure people: he may also have to fill in forms, keep accounts, tidy his consulting-room and all sorts of other things. But we (rightly) have the feeling that there is some enterprise with which these people are, or ought to be, specially connected, something that is central to what they do. Just as doctors are concerned primarily with medicine and promoting health, so (we may feel) teachers and others are, or ought to be, primarily engaged in the enterprise of educating.

This feeling, so far vaguely expressed, does not allow us to conclude that the other enterprises are unimportant or ought somehow to be got rid of. Plainly, much will depend on

circumstance. If we are attacked by barbarians or have not enough
to eat, it will no doubt be sensible for teachers (and perhaps even
doctors) to stop teaching (curing) and turn their attention to
finding food for themselves and other people or to fending off
enemy attacks. The feeling is rather that there are *in principle* —
'in theory' if you like, though we hope also in practice — enterprises
whose nature just *is* different. Educating people is one thing;
curing them is another; keeping them properly fed is yet another;
and so on. We have different words that fairly mark these
enterprises ('education', 'medicine', 'economics'), but the words in
themselves may not give us a sufficient grasp of what the enterprises
are and how they differ from each other. For the enterprises exist
in their own right ('in principle' or 'in theory'), whether or not
people identify them clearly with certain words. Even if people did
not identify them or practise them at all, they would still be
important: the enterprises we call 'science', 'medicine', and
'democracy' are important in themselves, even though many
societies may have had no understanding of them and lived by
superstition, witch-doctoring and tyranny.

There are two general temptations that need special notice. The
first lies in identifying an enterprise that exists in its own right with
particular social practices or institutions. To take a parallel: human
beings may engage in an activity or enterprise that we may want to
call 'religion' (though, no doubt, we are not entirely clear just what
this enterprise is). It would be wrong to think that this is the same
as saying that certain people and social practices — parsons,
funerals, churches and so on — actually exist or even that there
are certain sets of beliefs and doctrines which are called 'religious'.
For we could always ask, 'Are these people (institutions, beliefs,
etc.), whatever they may be called, actually concerned with
religion?', and we may often find that they are not. If we identify
religion with certain social practices, we make the same mistake as
the man who is humorously quoted as saying, 'When I say religion
of course I mean the Christian religion, and when I say the
Christian religion of course I mean the Church of England.' The
point is not just that the man is prejudiced: it is that he has no idea
of religion as an enterprise in its own right.

So it is with the notion of educating people. We may call certain
things 'schools' and certain people 'teachers'; and we may say that
what we are doing is to educate children, but we have to be able to

show that this is, in fact, what we are doing. The mere existence of social practices with the word 'education' attached to them indicates nothing; any more than, in the police state of Orwell's *1984* the existence of an institution called 'The Ministry of Truth' proved that the institution was, in fact, concerned with truth (rather than, as Orwell represents it, with propaganda). It is a very open question how much actual education goes on in those institutions that we currently classify under that heading. Clearly, we cannot answer the question until we know, or decide, what 'education' is to signify; but equally we cannot assume that the answer is provided by existing institutions.

The second temptation is to use (or abuse) 'education' to endorse not a particular set of social practices but some particular ideal or set of values that we happen to favour. Most writers on the subject have some general ideology, or 'doctrine of man', or political or moral theory that they want to sell, and their 'educational theory' (together with what they want 'education' to mean) exists chiefly as a kind of spin-off, so to speak, from this general ideal. Thus Plato (*Laws*, 643—4):

> When we abuse or commend the upbringing of individual people and say that one of us is educated and the other uneducated, we sometimes use this latter term of men who have in fact had a thorough education — one directed towards petty trade or the merchant shipping business, or something like that. But I take it that for the purpose of the present discussion we are not going to treat this sort of thing as 'education'; what we have in mind is education from childhood in *virtue,* a training which produces a keen desire to become a perfect citizen who knows how to rule and be ruled as justice demands. I suppose we should want to mark off this sort of upbringing from others and reserve the title 'education' for it alone.

A very large part of Plato's 'educational theory', in the *Republic* and elsewhere, is devoted to this particular goal: that is, to turning out 'perfect citizens' in the interests of a well ordered state.

It is worth noticing here that it is not just the English word 'education' that tempts us to move in one or the other of these two directions. Other words in other languages suffer the same fate: thus Plato, in the passage above, monopolizes the Greek word *paideia* (here translated as 'education') for his particular purposes, and the same can be, and has been, done with the French *éducation,* the German *Bildung* and so forth. The same temptations beset words (in any language) that signify enterprises of a fairly general nature, which we have not taken the trouble to get clear: 'religion', 'politics', 'morals' and many others. They lure us to endorse either existing social practices or else our own partisan views (and, indeed, these two may obviously be connected with each other more closely than we have here made apparent).

So far as we can see, these and other similar manoeuvres are not only mistaken but largely unnecessary. As has been suggested elsewhere (Wilson, 1979b), there is a concept that, when properly explained, makes tolerably clear the kind of enterprise we need to distinguish and (though this is, in one way, a secondary consideration) best fits the term 'educate' as it is now normally used by English-speakers (and other parallel terms that exist in other languages). To state this as briefly as possible: 'education' is the marker for a particular enterprise or activity, which has as its aim or 'good' the sustained and serious learning of rational creatures, planned in some coherent or overall way. We educate people (rather than treating them in other ways) when we are engaged in bringing such learning about, and people become educated when, or in so far as, they have done some learning of the kind.

Compared with the particular pictures presented by most authors, this is a fairly broad concept, but it is, we think, the concept that most contemporary English-speakers mark by the term 'education'. There is some limitation on what learning will count as education. We do not use the term of trivial or fragmentary bits of learning, nor of the learning of animals or infants, but we do use it where what is learned may be undesirable (bad habits, hatred of Jews or plenty of other things) and where the amount of knowledge or understanding is very small (one can learn, in a serious and sustained way, to acquire certain habits, or skills, or attitudes without much knowledge attached to them). We speak of *bad* (that is, not just incompetent but evil) education — just as we can speak of bad religion, bad moral principles, bad political ideals and so on: we have to distinguish these from cases that are not cases of religion, or morality, or politics at all — and also of education that does not involve much knowledge or understanding.

This (very brief) sketch needs to be supplemented by two

elaborations. First, some limitation, not so much of content as of
general intention, is placed on the concept of education by virtue
of the fact that education is a general or comprehensive kind of
enterprise. Thus the Oxford English Dictionary speaks of
'education' as 'systematic instruction, schooling or training', and
for 'educate' gives 'to bring up (young persons) from childhood so
as to form [their] habits, manners, intellectual and physical
aptitudes'. Not just any learning counts as education; the learning
has to be seen as part of a systematic and coherent enterprise.
Hence the grammar of 'to educate' is different from the grammar
of (for instance) 'to train'. We can train people in particular skills,
or for particular tasks, or as fillers of particular roles, but we can
only educate *people as such*: if we claim to educate people, we
claim to be viewing their learning from some general, overall or
comprehensive point of view, not *just* with an eye to certain jobs or
skills.

Of course, since people have minds, and since education consists
of learning, it is likely that a large part of this enterprise will be
seen as the development of knowledge and understanding in
people; indeed, an educational ideal that involved no such
development would be hard to conceive. Yet one might easily
think that the really important things for people to learn — still in
a comprehensive and coherent sort of way — did not involve much
intellectual or 'cognitive' sophistication but were more in the area
marked by 'character', 'habits', 'attitudes' and so forth; and one
might believe that these things were best learned by imitation, or
practice, or exhortation, or games-playing or other methods of that
kind. Again, one might think it rash to lay down any particular
content as being 'really important' for *all* pupils — such content
might reasonably vary according to each pupil's particular needs,
abilities or station in life. But the notion of education is neutral
with regard to any questions of content; so long as there is an
enterprise of this general kind, the term 'education' cannot be
rejected.

Second, 'education' is normally a fairly formal, structured or
institutionalized enterprise, something designed to raise people
above the level of what they would naturally learn for themselves
in the ordinary course of events. We do not speak of parents and
other language-users educating their children, or even teaching
them to talk, if the children just pick up the use of language from

the adults — even though this learning may be thought crucially important for any mental development. We may, indeed, loosely say that certain people or experiences exercise an 'educational' effect, but 'educate' is a much narrower term than 'bring up', 'rear' or 'nurture'.

These are at least some of the issues that would emerge from a thorough and systematic study of how words are actually used. Much more work, in our judgement, needs to be done in this field, both on English words and on those terms that are, at least *prima facie,* parallel in other natural languages. But whatever may or may not be true of English and other usage, the important point is: a particular kind of enterprise exists that needs to be delimited in this way because it is concerned with a certain kind of 'good' — namely, learning. There are, of course, still wider concepts: 'upbringing', say, or 'what we do for children' would include a number of very different goods: at one time we are concerned with our children's health, at another with their appearance and so on. Learning, though a broad enough idea, represents only one kind of interest; nor is this interest confined to children. A variety of other terms normally goes along with this particular interest; we would not refer to children as pupils, for instance, nor to adults as teachers unless we had this interest in mind.

There are other enterprises concerned with other specific goods, as we have already noted, and it is important to see that each of these is delimited or bounded in the same sort of way. Often this is clear to us: we know pretty well when we do something to a person for medical reasons, and we can distinguish these from educational or (say) economic reasons. A sick man may have to retire from attending university or from his business: this may be good for his health but bad for his education or his pocket. Sometimes, partly because of a lack of clarity about the terms and concepts in question, we are less clear. But whatever we choose to label as 'politics', or 'morals' or (to take a currently fashionable term) 'ideology', we must, if these terms are to have any clear meaning, be able to distinguish a political (moral, ideological) reason for doing something from another kind of reason, which means that we must be able to distinguish it from an educational reason.

In fact, if we resist the temptation to extend terms like 'political' ('moral', 'ideological', etc.) to cover more or less any consideration, we can already do this in many cases. It is politically desirable that when attacked by barbarians we should not worry too much about learning things but should devote our attention to keeping our society safe. It is morally desirable that if Romans are in danger of being burned alive, we should at least put off learning the violin until we have done what we can to help them. It is, or may be, 'ideologically' desirable (though we are not entirely clear what 'ideologically' means) that children from different social backgrounds should belong to the same school or the same housing estate; but whether this improves these children's learning may be another matter.

It is for these reasons that the concept of education, as we have tried to delimit it, cannot sensibly be seen as 'contestable', 'dependent on one's ultimate values' or anything of that kind, any more than can the concept of medicine, with its connected good (health). Indeed, we can go somewhat further than this. The enterprise of education is plainly necessary for any human society or individual, a point largely masked by those authors who prefer to adopt a much more stringent and value-impregnated concept and have to try to 'justify' it. The reason is that we could not come to resemble anything much like human beings or rational creatures unless we had done a good deal of serious and sustained learning, and it is implausible to suppose that such learning could be successfully done if it were left entirely to chance and nature. Some general or overall attempt, on a more or less broad front, to advance children's learning — whatever we may think it important to learn — seems essential if only because natural ability and circumstance are unreliable. In much the same way, an enterprise devoted to keeping people fit and healthy (that is, medicine) will be an inevitable feature of almost any society, even if different societies vary in their ideas of what counts as fitness or health, as they certainly vary in their ideas of how to achieve it.

Whether or not this sort of delimitation is acceptable as a definition of education does not ultimately matter all that much as long as we are clear about, and agree on, what verbal markers we are attaching to which enterprises. Few people will deny the importance of sustained and serious learning, even though they might dispute the delimitation, and even though they might disagree about what ought to be learned. But we are not always as clear as we should be about the logical or conceptual requirements that the notion of sustained and serious learning itself imposes on us and that we have to attend to if our educational practice is to prosper (Wilson, 1977). There is a real danger that, under pressure from other (non-educational) sources, teachers and educators may lose their grip on what must surely be regarded as central at least to the notion of education.

There are two general ways in which an enterprise can be corrupted: by external pressure and by internal corruption.

(1) External Pressure

It may be that because of external pressures or desires that conflict with the enterprise, 'society' — or some group of power holders — does not give the necessary powers to those who should be conducting it. In so far as the Communist Party tells biologists what they are to think, or painters how they are to paint, to that extent biology and painting become corrupted. If administrators and porters do not allow doctors the scope and power necessary to conduct operations and otherwise treat their patients as the doctors think best, to that extent medicine is impossible. Similarly, if there is no class of people who are empowered to educate — who are charged with the making of educational decisions and trusted to use the time and money involved as they think best without fear of outside pressure — education bcomes difficult or impossible. If a Gestapo agent, or a Party commissar, or a 'democratic consensus', or an educational fashion, or parental or bureaucratic pressure is breathing down the educator's neck and telling him what to do, he cannot do his job satisfactorily. The position becomes impossible for the enterprise, just as chess-playing cannot flourish if politicians tell chess-players what moves to make.

It has been argued elsewhere (Wilson, 1977) that the people most plausibly to be identified as educators, and therefore to be given the relevant powers, are the *teachers* (in schools and universities) because, briefly, they have a better grasp of the knowledge and other things to be learned and they are personally familiar with the students who are doing the learning. We do not, of course, deny that both parents and society have some rights here — for instance, to insist that students at least learn to be economically and socially viable — but within certain fairly obvious limits the enterprise must be conducted by those on the spot and in the know. The educators must have whatever disciplinary powers they need: sufficient powers to order the curriculum, the organization of the school and the methods of teaching; powers over the spending of whatever money society can afford to devote to education; powers to ensure the sanctity and potency of the school (college, university), if necessary in the teeth of society or political pressures; and powers to ensure the educability of their pupils (which include at least certain powers over the home environment). All these seem notoriously lacking in our society — and, indeed, in any society we know of (see chapter 7).

(2) Internal Corruption

Even if these powers are granted, it is always possible, of course, that the educators themselves may lose a proper grip on their own enterprise. They may become — as many clearly have become — corrupted by various types of irrationality. A very great deal of what passes for 'educational theory' or 'educational research' betrays this corruption. It arises chiefly from various fantasies about the human mind, which issue in forms that are, or should be, well-known (Wilson, 1979a): a belief in behaviourism and 'behavioural objectives', the regarding of almost any attribute as a 'skill', an addiction to sociology and ideology, an obsession with egalitarianism and social class, and the characteristically liberal guilt feeling that makes us dismiss or play down ideas marked by 'punishment', 'examination', 'competition' and 'segregation' (ideas that at root encapsulate necessary features of any serious learning and any serious institution devoted to learning).

Human beings are, we think, susceptible to these fantasies and types of irrationality in any social system; indeed, social systems usually do no more than echo and institutionalize the types of fantasy to which all individuals are liable. It is important to ensure that the external pressures are checked in order that education may have at least the chance of flourishing; but it is equally important that the tendencies to internal corruption are also checked in order that it may actually flourish. For that reason we believe that, however much light may be shed on the external, sociological or institutional forces that make education difficult, these forces will continue to flourish in one form or another so

long as the basic fantasies continue to dominate us. It thus seems
to be ultimately itself an educational issue; enough influential
individuals need to understand the nature of the enterprise and its
necessary conditions, and to gain sufficient control over their
fantasies, to ensure that their intellects do not renege on what they
have learned philosophically. This applies particularly to teachers
themselves.

It is not surprising that education is today a natural stamping-
ground both for political and bureaucratic pressure and for inner
irrationality: there are obvious reasons why education attracts
both the earnest technologically-minded bureaucrat and the
pseudo-idealist acting out his own compulsions. The really tiresome
thing about this is that it masks the extent to which education, if
allowed and encouraged to flourish, could change things for the
better: an intuition that the 'great educators' of the past at least
kept alive. If we could really teach people not only to be socially
viable but also to become seriously attached to what is worth
while, to conduct their moral lives with at worst competence and
at best imagination and enthusiasm, to be able genuinely to love at
least some other people (if only their own children), to find some
genuine joy, excitement and contentment in life — if we could do
any or all of these things, we should at least have some idea of the
enormous power that education has in principle. That it does not
wield this power in practice is not, we are sure, due primarily to
intellectual incompetence, lack of research or lack of economic or
technological resources; it is due to the fact that we do not give the
enterprise a fair chance.

Hence it is difficult, in this present age, to say very much about
the positive possibilities of education: these sound futuristic or
Utopian. In much the same way, it would have been difficult in the
Middle Ages to talk of the 'wonders of science' or to make clear
what benefits the properly constituted and fantasy-free practice of
medicine would bring, because at that time these two enterprises
were hemmed about with enemies that made their proper practice
impossible. So it is with education now: it is apparent, here and
there (in those rare cases where educators are both properly
empowered and themselves uncorrupted), just how enormous are
the benefits it can bring. In a (real if imprecise) sense, anyone who
has ever had a loving parent or teacher knows well enough what
education can do. But such cases are, regrettably, rare: we do not

see many teachers with the influence of Socrates or Dr Arnold.
(Who would hire Socrates nowadays? And would Thomas Arnold
have tolerated the administrators and bureaucrats of today?) We
have, as it were, a vague if precious glimpse of what education
might be, if given a fair chance. That glimpse is worth hanging on
to, though perhaps not much is gained by singing hymns to it.
What we have to do, first and foremost, is to clear the ground — to
make the enterprise possible; then we will have some chance of
studying it, and conducting it, sensibly.

3

Studying Education

There are, on the one hand, theoretical or theory-based enterprises, such as medicine or engineering. Both these are backed by a solid body of scientific knowledge, and the criteria of success in each case are clear: patients get better or die, bridges stand up or fall down. Consequently, the standards and the nature of authority in these enterprises are also clear; we know, pretty well, what counts as being a good doctor, or professor of medicine, or engineer. On the other hand, there are strictly practical enterprises, such as sailing boats, or making pots, or riding horses; and though there may not be much (or any) theory behind these, it is still clear what counts as doing them well. Whether by innate skill, or practice, or some kind of unexplained magic, some people sail boats and ride horses faster than others or make pots that we think beautiful. But there are also many enterprises for which the standards of success are not as clear. Consider the enterprises of making a happy marriage, or being a good parent, or a social welfare worker, or a minister of the Church, or a counsellor. Conducting these enterprises well is not, or not primarily, a matter of learning more theory, of reading giant books on marriage or parenthood or the sociology of the family; nor is it just a matter of practical experience, of getting the knack or acquiring the flair that good sailors or horsemen or potters have. (Some people get worse the more experience and practice they have.) Education is one such enterprise.

So in what does success consist? Well, obviously, it has a lot to do with the sort of person you are; but this is rather too vague and suggests that good educators are entirely born and not made. One can learn to be a good educator, but this is not just a matter of learning a lot of 'theory' or getting a lot of 'practice'; nor is it some mixture of the two. It is learning to see things and understand things in certain ways, to be clear-headed, to have the courage or nerve to do what you think is right for education, to understand your own and other people's feelings, to be confident without arrogance, to be sensitive to the meanings of words and actions: and, not least, to appreciate the importance and difficulties of what you are going to teach, or of the forms of life in which you are going to educate children. That still sounds vague, and so (by comparison with, say, becoming a good engineer or sailor) it is. But the truth is this: we know that the best parents, ministers, educators and so on have a set of fairly *general* virtues, intellectual and practical and moral. Learning to be a good educator is learning to acquire these virtues.

Practising teachers, or people who are being trained to be teachers, are nowadays in a particularly difficult position. On the one hand, they have to (or will have to) cope with the practical task of teaching children and adolescents, many of whom may be stupid, ignorant, badly behaved or actually delinquent. On the other, they are constantly subjected to a stream of talk and writing about education produced by psychologists and sociologists and various other kinds of -ologists; and some of them may have to pass examinations in these -ologies. Either of these tasks would be difficult enough in itself; but to do both, and to relate one to another, needs almost superhuman powers.

In this position the teacher may adopt various right and wrong attitudes. It is worth while to try to identify them. First, he (she) may be over-impressed by what 'theorists' and 'researchers' of one kind or another do and may believe that 'the research findings show' or that 'sociology has proved' all sorts of things (say, about streaming and setting, or new ways of teaching English, or working-class cultures, or comprehensive schools, or the Piagetian 'stages of learning', or whatever). Second, he may think that what the theorists do is a total waste of time, probably because it seems of no use at all when he is actually coping with live children in a school. This is a common opinion among students who have recently finished some theoretical examination in education (a degree, a diploma or whatever) and have just started the practical job of teaching. Third, he may think (or at least talk and act as if he thought) that the only 'answer' to problems and difficulties in education lies in adopting and promoting some particular 'philosophy' or in joining some movement — for instance, 'deschooling', or 'breaking down subject barriers', or 'making teaching relevant to the modern world'. He may find himself deploring 'middle-class values', or pressing for 'better academic standards', or advocating 'the abolition of corporal punishment' or 'free schools'.

All these three attitudes, though quite understandable, are (mostly) wrong. The first is wrong because (as soon as one starts thinking about it carefully and critically) it is fairly clear that we actually know very little about education. 'Research' has not told us much, and most of its so-called 'findings' are questionable. There are very few first-rate people in the field of educational research or theory: the field is a very difficult one, and the way in which a great deal of psychological and sociological research has been done is open to devastating criticism. These are strong words but defensible (see Wilson, 1972), and our first piece of advice to teachers is that they should not allow themselves to.be conned by incompetent theorists. They should adopt a highly critical attitude to all 'theory' and 'research', use their common sense and powers of logic and not be bullied by the technical terms and jargon.

The second is also wrong, in a way. For although it is true that most research is (a) of no use to the practising teacher in the classroom and (b) in itself badly done and invalid (and note that (a) and (b) are two different criticisms), it does not follow that the whole idea of doing research and finding things out is a total waste of time. We are in the very early stages of educational theory and research, and it may be some time before we learn how to do it better, so that it pays off. After all, this has been true of theory and research in most areas — the beginnings of research in science and mathematics and medicine were not obviously of much use; later on they were seen to be essential. So what we have to do is not to abandon the whole idea of thinking harder about education or 'researching' into it but to learn to think about it more intelligently.

The third attitude is wrong because it is basically a way of avoiding having to think about education intelligently. It is much easier to adopt some kind of cause, to join a movement, to use various slogans ('breaking down subject barriers, deschooling', etc.), than to think hard and critically. With some people this almost takes the shape of religious faith: what they believe in does not rest on evidence, or on any objective and careful consideration of problems, but is generated by some kind of desire or fantasy that has very little to do with the real world. It is like joining some kind of religious sect: you become a 'follower of so-and-so's methods', a 'progressive' and so on. Most discussion about education is a blend of religious and political argument (which is why it is usually so boring).

What we have to do, then (corresponding to the three mistakes above), is (1) keep a clear head and not be talked into swallowing what theorists say whole; (2) retain a general and serious interest in education and its problems — that is, not give up the whole thing as a bad job; and (3) consider each problem carefully for what it is rather than sweeping everything under the mat of a particular religion, political outlook or fashionable educational ideal. We have to take a big step backwards, *out of* the besieging world of talk and writing and 'movements' and 'theories'; we have to shake off all the things that are topical, or fashionable, or popular, or second-hand. Then — only then — will we have a fighting chance; otherwise we are just the mouthpieces of whatever climate of opinion happens to be prevalent.

This is not easy. One does not need to be very clever to do it, and certainly one does not need to have read a lot of books by educationalists. What one needs is courage, patience and a clear head — above all, a clear head — an unwillingness to tolerate nonsense, jargon, prejudice, journalistic chit-chat, high-minded statements about the 'aims of education' and anything phoney, anything that is not clear and genuine, anything that does not make sense. Most educational writing, on these counts, is not to be tolerated. We need to get things straight in a down-to-earth way, not to wander about among long words or pretty images or powerful prejudices.

Perhaps this is a good point at which to say that this book is not intended primarily as something for the reader to *agree* with. Naturally, we hope he may agree with some of it, but what matters is that it should help him to clarify what he thinks. If it is understandable and gives him something clear to *dis*agree with, that is just as good. What is important is the thinking, the arguing, the dialogue that one conducts with other people and/or inside one's own head. The reader should not either agree or disagree because he likes or dislikes the *idea* of what is being said or because it is unpalatable, unfashionable or contrary to what he has been taught or because it fits his prejudices; he should produce *reasons* and *arguments*. In a short book of this kind there will be plenty of points at which things could be disputed, so he can disagree with it as much as he likes. What is essential is that he should not react to anything because it sounds 'authoritarian', or 'traditional', or 'progressive'; indeed, part of the point of the book is to try to stop ourselves from thinking in that kind of way. We have to consider what is actually said and the reasons for and against it.

This has something to do with 'philosophy', but we should not be deceived by the word. Certainly, it has nothing at all to do with adopting a 'philosophy' of education (that is, being converted to some movement or creed). Indeed, philosophy — we would rather just say 'thinking seriously about what is said' — is a battle against this. It is a matter of being sufficiently serious and critical and clear-headed when one talks — or when one hears or reads other people talking and writing — about anything that is 'abstract' and complicated (as education certainly is), a matter of not saying just anything, or of letting other people get away with saying just anything, but of *meaning* what one says and not being satisfied until it is really clear. This is not an exercise that teaches 'facts' and 'answers': it is something which one learns by doing it and seeing other people do it.

A lot of meaning is packed into a phrase we have just used, 'being sufficiently serious'. We do not mean 'earnest' (as opposed to 'flippant'): people can be very earnest (as Hitler was) and quite mad. 'Seriousness' is the opposite of 'fantasy' and 'prejudice'; it is the reverse of 'living in a dream', 'believing and saying just anything', being 'out of touch with the real world'. The serious person, confronted with most writings on education, will not jump right in and say, 'Yes, how I agree!', or 'No, I don't like the sound of that.' He will want to spend a lot of time on two questions: what on earth does this chap actually mean? And is it true? These questions represent real or serious worries; other reactions — when one feels tempted just to jump in — reflect the fact that one is being pushed around by a fantasy or prejudice. We need to keep a constant watch on ourselves to detect when we are being serious and when we are merely reacting under the influence of fantasy.

In this book we shall be concerned chiefly with this kind of work. The reader may think, 'Isn't that making heavy weather of it? Surely we know well enough what we mean when we advance educational views and theories: we ought rather to get on with deciding whether they're true or right.' But do we really think that? Isn't that a sort of fantasy — a very convenient and pleasant one — that stops us facing the horrid fact that we do *not* know what we mean clearly enough? Of course, it is nasty and painful to realize that we are in a muddle: nevertheless, it is so. Consider a few words commonly flung around in education: 'child-centred', 'open-ended', 'accountability', 'autonomy', 'creativity', 'integration', 'relevance' and so on. Isn't it quite obvious that we are *not* clear what we mean? (Perhaps, indeed, the terms do not have any clear meaning.) And yet people happily use these words to promote and advertise various educational movements and practical policies when all the time they do not, in a literal sense, know what they are talking about.

These examples are all of semi-technical terms, and one awful thing about educational literature is that it has spawned a whole host of these. (Much of the trouble here comes from psychologists and sociologists: are we, are they, really clear what is meant by 'stage of development', 'heteronomy', 'divergent thinking', or even 'role', 'class', or 'culture'?) But exactly the same point applies to words that we might think we are clearer about because they are not technical but quite ordinary terms. Take phrases or words like 'teaching a subject', 'discipline', 'keeping order', 'motivation', 'values', 'religious education': *once we start to think* (and that is more than half the battle) we come to see that we are nothing like as clear as we thought we were. We are worried about some practical situation in school and express our worry by using the word 'discipline'. Well, just what is 'discipline'? What are we talking about when we talk about 'discipline'? (If the reader still thinks this is a silly question, or that the answer is obvious, he should look at chapter 4.)

However practical and down-to-earth our worries may be — and it is often best to start with a practical case, even if our interests are more wide-ranging and theoretical — we have to express these worries in language. We cannot help using phrases and words like 'good at English', 'punishment', 'motivation' and so on. They come

into our very description of the practical situation, and we shall
not get far even with describing our situations accurately unless we
take the words and phrases seriously. Understanding the words is,
in part, understanding the situations and seeing them more clearly.
It makes a difference, for instance, whether we see a pupil as
'naughty' or 'mentally ill'. What is the difference between these
two descriptions? What do we *mean by* each of them? To take
practical situations and real-life worries seriously involves taking
what we say about them seriously.

This is where our prejudices and fantasies get in the way. To
take an extreme example: suppose you are a passionate Marxist
(or something of the kind), and you see every situation in this
society as a case of 'oppression by the capitalist classes' and
everyone as 'a tool of the bourgeoisie'. This will obviously affect
your educational decisions and will prevent you from facing
particular problems with proper attention to detail. Or you may be
obsessed with the idea that the working-classes are being repressed,
or that children are being forced into trying to meet 'academic
standards' that are not 'relevant', or that the differences between
various school subjects are 'artificial', or that 'intrinsic' motivation
(whatever that is) should always be preferred to 'extrinsic' — or
practically anything.

Now, of course, this does not mean that what Marxists or others
say is silly. But — and this is where we use words like 'doctrinaire',
'obsessed', 'dominated by fantasy', etc. — there is an important
difference between the person who wants to fit everything into his
own way of seeing the world and the person who is prepared to
look at what we actually say and what the facts are. It is not so
much that one always wants to disagree with the first person:
maybe we are (in some cases) slaves of the capitalist classes and so
on. But there are other things to be said and noticed. We have to
fight free from the compulsion (all of us have this problem) to
force our own fantasies on to the world. Some cases of fantasy —
Hitler's and the Nazis' belief in the virtue of 'Aryan blood', for
instance — are obvious (though lots of educated Germans appeared
to believe such fantasies); others, particularly if they are topical, or
respectable, or in line with current educational opinion, are more
insidious.

Throughout this book we shall be struggling with various
fantasies, which tempt us (you, or me, or various writers on

education) to say muddled or silly things. It is a difficult business, but once one has acquired a taste for it, one begins to see just how much work we need to do here, and what a waste of time it is to go on talking or advancing theories or supporting movements when we are not *clear*. As we make progress, we find ourselves seeing in a different perspective problems that our fantasy at first forced us to see in only a single light: not 'the right' perspective or 'the right' answer, but rather a more sophisticated, more realistic, less *compulsive* view.

What may be of use to us, before we get down to particular topics in the book, is to be able to recognize particular fantasies. For instance, whenever we discuss rules and punishments (together with authority and discipline), there is a common feeling that some things — perhaps particularly punishment — are somehow 'bad' (cruel, unfair, unpleasant, to be avoided or at least to be apologized for). The question 'Why *should* we (they) be subjected to all this?' may be asked with truculence or with protective pity. People are reminded of harsh and unreasonable authorities (Victorian parents, Dickensian schoolteachers). This might be described as a very strong 'anti-authoritarian' fantasy. The feeling is, perhaps, that the whole of the rules/authority apparatus ought really to be dismantled or at least played down: that it ought to be replaced by something quite different ('love', 'concern', 'interest', or whatever). Curiously, even teachers who have a hard time surviving in very tough, undisciplined schools still manage to retain this fantasy — which shows, incidentally, how a fantasy with really deep roots will survive even the hardest knocks from the real world.

Or when we discuss integrating or segregating people, we may feel that there is something wrong with putting people into separate categories or compartments (setting, streaming, segregating): we ought rather to lump them all together in a nice, warm group or community, otherwise (the feeling is) we are making differences between human beings that we ought not to make, or emphasizing distinctions we ought not to emphasize. (Sometimes segregation is criticized as 'élitist' or 'divisive', whatever that means.) So we must have comprehensive education, mixed-ability groups and so on. Underlying this, perhaps, is the fear that to recognize and cater for differences between people must necessarily be to regard some people as superior or inferior to others in the eyes of God, so to speak; it is as if we did not really believe in the equality of *persons* at all, or did not think that our belief could stand up to a recognition of their different attributes.

Or, again, since the rise of the natural sciences (physics, chemistry, etc.) many people have developed a fantasy that human beings are amenable to the same sort of 'scientific' investigation — 'social science'. This is what underlies the exaggerated respect sometimes paid to psychology, sociology, social psychology, sociometry, psychometry and so on, as if computers, statistics, 'research findings' and all the apparatus that is at home in the physical (natural) sciences were also appropriate for dealing with people. It is not. Of course, there are many complex problems here, but the desire to be 'professional', 'expert', 'properly qualified', 'scientific' and so on has outstripped performance. This area operates as a kind of fantasy world with its own jargon, more like a carefully worked out superstition (astrology, for instance) than anything sensible.

Talk about 'relevance' often runs into fantasy. We all know, in our saner moments, that lots of things we learn (for instance, the enjoyment of Beethoven or Shakespeare) are good in themselves, not because they are 'relevant to the twentieth century' or anything of that kind, and that different school subjects represent real differences in the questions we want to ask and the interests we have. Yet a great deal of talk about making subjects 'relevant' or of 'breaking down subject barriers' betrays an ignorance or denial of this. Perhaps part of the (very strong) feeling here is a deep fear of making distinctions and noticing differences, as if everything would be much more warm and comfortable if only we merged everything into one rather than separating things out. 'Irrelevant' subjects are perhaps also alarming because we have to confront them in their own right — we cannot at once see their use or connect them with worries about 'society' or the 'modern world'.

Finally, there is a common fantasy — it has almost the status of a religious creed — that ascribes everything to, and connects everything with, 'society'. Pupils must be educated 'in terms of the society they live in' (but think again of enjoying Beethoven); it is 'our materialistic society', and not individuals, that is to blame for all sorts of evils; it is 'social conditioning' that has generated the subjection of women, racial prejudice, underprivileged minorities and so on. 'Society', in this fantasy, is the recipient and sponsor of almost all causes and effects, rather as God, the devil or human nature might have been in the past. Excessive dependence on sociology may encourage the spread of this fantasy, which perhaps arises from the unpleasantness of accepting individual responsibility, values that are not tied to any 'society' and culture-free reasoning in general. It is easier to cast all blame on 'society' than to think about its problems for oneself.

We should be surprised if the reader could not detect the operation of one or other of these fantasies either in his own thinking or in the talk and writing of other people. And in some cases he may well feel, 'What right have they got to call this a fantasy? It is perfectly reasonable — 'society' *is* to blame, divisions between subjects *are* artificial, punishment *is* a bad thing,' and so on. But, as we noted earlier, that is not quite the point. What the truth is — what we can correctly and reasonably say in each case — will emerge only after a lot of long, patient and careful discussion. (It is a fantasy in itself to think that the truth is obvious, and that one has arrived at it, and that no more need be said.) But we get at the truth more quickly when we are able to recognize (and thus lay aside) the extravagant things that fantasy makes us say. Thus we are able to recognize people who are obsessed with ideas (even if we happen to sympathize with those ideas), who do not just dislike the idea of punishment or subjects, as we may ourselves, but go wild and say, 'No rules in schools at all!' or 'There shouldn't be such things as subjects.' In such cases we shall think something like, 'Well, I sympathize with these feelings, but that's not quite the right way to put it', or 'but that's not the thing to say', and we shall try to get these people to express their feelings in a more appropriate form, so that they say what is true and correct rather than — so to speak — just *anything*. This business of marrying up feelings and statements is the only way in which we can do business at all. From a strictly professional point of view, it can be done just by paying immensely careful attention to what is said; but it is also helpful to have some idea of the feelings that make one say things, so that one can beware of being carried away by them.

Of course, there are plenty of other fantasies: we all have them, to a greater or lesser extent, and inevitably they emerge in our stated opinions. It might be valuable if from time to time in the course of working through this book the reader were to think about his feelings and natural attitudes, about why, really, he is

inclined to say this or that. One can do this profitably only by going
over the same ground again and again as one tries to get things
straight. In doing this one finds oneself backsliding sometimes, no
longer *thinking* but relapsing into feeling. (It can be very helpful to
use a tape-recorder when discussing: it becomes clear what sorts
of feelings and passions dominate our thoughts. One can replay
the tape of a discussion and discuss the same point again in a more
sophisticated and fantasy-free manner.)

But the important thing, both in reading what is written and in
listening to what we and others say, is to *attend to the words,* not to
react in some general way to the 'outlook' or the 'view'. If one does
the latter, one starts labelling opinions as 'élitist', 'authoritarian',
'progressive' and so on, and that is a waste of time. Only two issues
are at stake: is what is said *clear*? And is it *true*? There is the
strongest possible contrast here with the question of whether what
is said is fashionable, or forceful, or 'relevant'. If people do not
attend to each other's words and to their own, we have nothing
more than the mutual clashing of fantasies — which is, indeed,
what most so-called discussions actually consist of. This is an
advance on people actually fighting each other: but, in terms of
reaching the truth, not a very big one.

This does not mean that, as we make progress, our worries will
diminish. (Our fantasies should become less powerful, but that is
different.) For we will inevitably come to see that things are *not* so
clear; and then, if we care at all, we shall (rightly) feel worried
about making them clearer. We shall start thinking things like,
'Well, wait a minute, just what *is* "morality"? What actually do we
mean by "discipline" — is it the same as "keeping order"? We talk
of "love" and "concern", but what are we talking *about*? What are
"comprehensive" schools supposed to "comprehend"?' And so on.
Once we have got to this stage, we are in business, because we
want to get things straight — and then we are faced with an
enjoyable, if lengthy, task rather than an irrelevant or boring chore
or (because it might threaten some fantasy) a dangerous and
alarming risk. Ideally, one needs some *passion for clarity,* an
intolerance of muddle. Certainly, both the practical and the
theoretical aspects of education are muddled enough. That is why
getting clear is both the first and the most important task if we are
to achieve the right practical results.

The reader may now be thinking: 'This is supposed to be a

chapter about studying education, but all we have had is a sermon about not being prejudiced. What about the importance of psychology, or sociology, or philosophy, or history, or educational research, and all the other scholarly things we have been told about (and perhaps have to pass examinations in)?' We have two answers to this. First, we discuss these disciplines in other chapters (particularly chapter 10); secondly, and more important, the reader should at least begin by making *absolutely no assumptions* about the value, methodology or alleged success of this or that discipline (psychology or whatever) or its relevance to practical education. When — but only when, and the time is a long way off — we are all really clear just what psychologists and others are trying to say, whether and how it can be verified and what use practical educators could make of it, then (and not till then) we shall be in a position to talk of solid chunks of knowledge that, as conscientious students, we shall no doubt wish to learn off by heart. Until then it is wisest to strive only for common sense and clarity. We hope the following chapters will make that programme seem more plausible.

Part II

4

Discipline and Authority

Perhaps the first real worry teachers have (even before they start teaching) is about how to keep order, or maintain discipline, or in general control their pupils. If they are not worried about this, they ought to be: because obviously one has to have some degree of control or order or organization whatever one may want to do with and for the pupils. This remains true however nice or co-operative they are and however easy-going the teacher may want to be. This does not apply only to teachers: it applies to anybody whose job consists of getting people to do things or of doing things for people. An army officer has to get his soldiers to train and fight and march, and he needs the kind of discipline that is necessary for this purpose. A boss in business has to get his secretaries and subordinates to do what has to be done in order to keep the business running. A doctor has to insist that certain rules are enforced if he is to be able to conduct operations, make diagnoses and so on.

We might think, 'Yes, that's all very true, but why should *thinking* about "discipline" or "authority" help? Surely, either you're the sort of person who is good at keeping order (or you become that sort of person by practice and experience) or you're not; and either you're dealing with pupils who are reasonably well behaved or you're not. You can't improve things by thinking.' Or we might be prepared to say, 'Perhaps some kinds of thinking or "research" might help us: for instance, perhaps a sociologist or a psychologist or a very experienced teacher could tell us that we'd keep better order if (say) we spoke more loudly, or didn't use "middle-class vocabulary", or weren't so "authoritarian", or taught sometimes from the back of the classroom. But how can it help to think about *what it is* to "have authority" or to "keep discipline"? What's the point of considering the 'philosophy' of all this? We know already what we're talking about: our difficulties are purely practical.'

We hope to show that this is a mistake — and not only that, but a very important kind of mistake. The mistake is (putting it roughly) to think that *we already know clearly enough what we are trying to do,* so that (it seems) all we need is practical help in doing it. Of course, sometimes this is the position. If we want to cure someone of lumbago, we know well enough what we are trying to do: we just need somebody to tell us the right techniques. But what about 'curing schizophrenia' — is it as clear what would count as 'curing' it, or even what 'schizophrenia' is? Again, we know more or less what we are talking about when we say we want to teach children their tables or how to spell, but what about teaching 'morality'? What is it to 'teach morality'? In education, as we hope to show in this and other chapters, it is usually the case that we are *not* clear about what we are trying to do. There are muddles and vaguenesses around the notions of 'discipline', 'authority', and so on, which make them good examples to start with, not least because they represent severely practical concerns.

One possible muddle is this. When we use words like 'discipline', 'keeping order' and so on, we may be interested in two different things. Both are necessary to effective teaching and learning (or to any other operation involving people), but they are different. First, there is the business of organizing whatever we are doing. For instance, in an army an officer may arrange for a guard to be set at certain hours, or he may deploy his troops in certain positions; in a hospital a surgeon may arrange that the nurse holds the swabs and scalpels ready, that there is silence in the operating theatre and so on. Secondly, there is the different matter of people's acceptance of our arrangements. The troops might mutiny, or the nurse may fail to turn up on time for the operation.

The word 'discipline' fits the second of these two concerns rather than the first. The discipline of an army or a hospital may be bad even though the organization and arrangements are (on paper, so to speak) quite good. The hospital may have a superb timetable and all the latest modern equipment and be staffed by the most expert doctors and nurses, but if the people are too lazy or moody or impulsive to keep the rules, the organization will not be much use. (Conversely, a very well disciplined body of people may fail because there is no proper organization.)

What we are talking about here, then, is not just any kind of 'keeping order'. Discipline has to do with the reactions and behaviour of people to rules — roughly, with whether they obey them or not. This is different from 'organization', and it is also different from a number of other things that might be confused with it. For instance, it is not the same as morale, or confidence, or being cheerful. The morale of an army may be very high, but it may be too undisciplined to be successful, like the confidently charging barbarians who fell before the well-disciplined Roman legions. So too an army could be very well-disciplined without necessarily being very optimistic or happy or cheerful — the troops might just plod doggedly and obediently on.

If we ask about the discipline in a classroom or in a body of pupils, then, we are asking about something fairly specific. We do not want to know whether a class is well-planned or well-organized, or whether the pupils are happy and cheerful; we want to know *whether the rules are obeyed*. It does not matter, from this particular point of view, what the rules actually *are*; what matters, in terms of discipline, is whether they are kept, or whether the pupils are too disobedient, mutinous, bloody-minded or rebellious to keep them. To say that discipline is about the pupils' attitude to the rules is not precise enough: they may think the rules silly or unpleasant and may very much want them changed — but they may still keep them, so that the discipline is all right.

Already we have distinguished one particular problem or area of interest — that which attaches to the specific notion of 'discipline' — from other areas. It is important to be able to tolerate (we hope, welcome) this procedure and not to be distracted by the other areas. Of course, these other areas matter: but they are different. It obviously matters, for instance, *what* the rules are: clearly, we want sensible rules, rules that will suit what we are trying to do (in this case, to teach the pupils something), and this needs more discussion. But that is a different matter from whether the rules, whatever they are, are obeyed or disobeyed. Different again is the question of whether pupils are happy and enthusiastic (whether or not the rules are sensible, and whether or not they are obeyed).

We have a variety of problems or interests here, and we have to keep them separate, otherwise we shall have little chance of solving any of them. There is a constant temptation to seek one single solution to a whole range of different phenomena ('bad discipline', 'lack of order', 'lesson refusal', 'disobedience', 'bad behaviour' and so on). We have to resist this temptation.

We are going to leave on one side, for the time being, these other questions — in particular, questions about what sort of rules we ought to have for pupils to obey. Let us just take it for granted — though it is obviously not always and everywhere true — that, by and large, we have a sensible set of rules for our pupils, rules, let us say, that are absolutely necessary if we are to get any education done and that pupils ought to stick to. Even then we have problems about discipline. For, plainly, unless all our pupils are angels, they will not always want to stick to all the rules.

Again, we might be tempted to say, 'But aren't these just practical problems? Isn't it just a matter of what actually works? We know clearly enough what we want now — good discipline: all we need is to find out how to get it.' But this is still too impatient. We have seen that classroom 'discipline' involves the notion of 'obeying rules' (and not other notions, like being well-organized or happy). But the notion of 'obeying rules' is not as clear as we might think.

Suppose that Julius Caesar commands a body of Roman soldiers who adore him and will do anything he tells them to. He lays down rules for them, which they obey out of love for him, so that we might want to say, 'What a well-disciplined body of men!' But now suppose Caesar is ill or dies; as soon as another general takes over, the soldiers immediately stop obeying all the rules because they do not admire the new general in the same way. Do we now say, 'What a badly-disciplined body of men!'? Or do we say 'They were never really well-disciplined in the first place. They obeyed Caesar's rules, true, but that was only because they loved him. Look what happens when there's a change of commander!'?

We might say either of these two things; what is important is to be clear about the difference. Take another example. Suppose a beautiful blonde teacher teaches a class of boys, and they are all half in love with her, so that they obey all the rules she gives them. Has she succeeded in 'establishing good discipline'? Well, in a sense obviously she has: the boys do actually obey. But the reasons for their obedience are a bit suspicious. It is not that there is anything wrong with boys feeling attracted to beautiful blondes, but we have the feeling that they should not be obeying for that reason. It is as if they are obeying the rules only by accident or on the side, so to speak: and we are not sure whether that is enough for us to talk about 'good discipline'.

So there seem to be two different actions that the teacher has to take, even within the notion of 'discipline' or 'obeying rules'. The first, which is important in itself, might be described as just *getting the rules obeyed,* without minding about the reasons for obedience. In principle (and sometimes in practice) this can be done in all sorts of ways — by keeping the pupils so interested in the subject that they do not want to disobey, or by teaching them so quickly and effectively that they do not have time to disobey, or by being a beautiful or fascinating person whom they admire, or by terrorizing them, or whatever. The second action, which is also important, is getting the pupils to obey rules *for the right reasons.* This second purpose is a bit more complicated, because clearly you have got to know what the right reasons are yourself; you have to get the pupils to understand them; and you have to persuade the pupils to use them to govern their behaviour.

The aims of these two actions are different. The first is pretty down-to-earth; we need what we might call 'law and order' so that we can get things done. We do not have to ensure much understanding on the part of the pupils as long as the rules are in fact kept. But in the second case — and this is why teachers and educators are in a special position — we are trying to educate the pupils. In running an army the job is to defeat the enemy, and as long as the soldiers keep whatever rules are necessary for this, it may not matter very much *why* they keep them (though we want to be able to rely on them to go on keeping them under various conditions, such as a change of commander). But in teaching and educating part of the job is precisely to change pupils' minds and the reasons why they do things: and the reasons why they keep (or break) rules come into this.

Suppose we start by considering the second case. We need to know the reasons why pupils (or anyone) should keep rules, and it is important to remember here that we are talking about *keeping rules* and the reasons for doing so, not about reasons why pupils should like their teachers, or be interested in their subject, or approve of their school in general, or 'conform to society' or anything else. It is fairly clear that there are two sorts of satisfactory reason for (say) keeping rules about telling the truth or not hitting other people. First, these and other rules are necessary for one particular purpose (education) or perhaps for many purposes (there could not be much interaction between human beings if there were not *some* adherence to the rule about telling the truth). So, many of the rules in schools ought to be kept because they are necessary for education — and we might note here, though it is not strictly relevant, that those who make the rules should do so on this basis. Secondly, rules should be kept *because they are rules,* even if (sometimes) we do not think they are sensible. When we say 'because they are rules', we do not mean just because they appear in a rule book: we mean that if they are really rules (and not just arbitrary impositions), they are backed by some kind of accepted authority — like Parliament, or the general of an army, or the head of a hospital, or (in our case) a teacher, head teacher or local authority of education.

Of course, if the authority is not accepted or agreed — if, for instance, there is a political *coup* and we suddenly find ourselves ruled by a dictator whom most people do not want — then this reason is no longer a good reason. We might want to start a revolution. In such a case the ruler would not really be an authority; he would just have power. 'Authority' implies that the power is legal, or agreed, or generally accepted, or legitimate. The authority of teachers, by and large, is plainly legitimate in this sense: they have a mandate given them by society to make the rules in schools for their pupils (though one might question the extent of the mandate and the wisdom of the rules they actually make).

So if we spelled out what ought to go on in the head of somebody faced with a rule — the sort of reason he ought to use — it might go something like this: 'Well, this *is* a rule: that is, it's been clearly laid down by a person (or committee) with authority. As a member of this society, I am under this authority and accept it, so I'll have to obey it.' Without some such consideration, it would obviously be impossible to have any sort of society or institution or interacting group of human beings at all because people can only interact and co-operate by agreeing to accept certain rules and procedures, and this involves the whole apparatus of authorities, rules, sanctions, punishments and so on. Of course, other things also happen in societies and institutions — people like or love each other, help each other, are more or less happy and interested in certain things — but here we are pin-pointing one set of things, the rules—authority—punishment set, which no society can do without.

In a way, the 'because it's a rule' reason for obedience is more important than the 'because it's sensible' reason; for the attitude of someone who says, 'I'll do whatever's sensible' is not good enough for discipline. It would be no good having soldiers who did only what they thought was sensible and necessary: soldiers must be unquestioningly obedient. We need to have pupils who see the point not just of particular (sensible) rules, but of the whole business of having an authority and sticking to the rules that the authority lays down. In fact, this point is pretty obvious in some contexts: on a sailing ship, for example, you have to have a captain and obey him (whether or not he makes mistakes), and generally there is no time for discussion or setting up committees. But in any context, even if one wants to have a great deal of discussion and consultation and participation, there is always a point at which there must be rules and an authority. In (some) schools it is easier to miss this point than it is on ships or in the army, where we cannot afford the luxury of debate and discussion.

Educating pupils in discipline, then, consists primarily of getting them to see this point: to see the force of the 'because it's a rule' reason. Note how very far removed this is from any idea of 'keeping order' by trying to be popular, or strict, or 'democratic', or 'authoritarian' as a teacher, or indeed by keeping the pupils interested or making their learning 'relevant'. For these would all be bad reasons for keeping rules ('because Miss So-and-so is so strict' or 'so nice'), whereas we have failed if we do not get across the good reason of 'because it's a rule'. The crucial point about this reason, which is the crucial point of discipline, is that it is *impersonal*: it does not depend on the pupils' liking the teacher or the particular rule; it depends solely on their respecting the rule *as a rule*. (One could think of ways of giving pupils practice in this, and assessing them, by setting up situations in which all other factors except a rule's being a rule pulled the other way: then we could see if they still obeyed it or not. If they did not, we would suspect that in other cases it was not its being a rule that really counted with them but something else — they wanted to do it anyway, or liked the teacher, or whatever).

Let us now go back to an earlier point and consider the teacher's task not of educating the pupils to keep rules for the right reasons but simply of getting the rules kept — of establishing 'law and order', so to speak. Having done some justice to the other, educational task, we might feel tempted to say, 'Well, it doesn't matter at all what methods we use to maintain "law and order", so long as they are efficient and don't do the pupils any real damage. If we can do it by being "nice" or "interesting" (or "strict" and "severe"), let's do that: if we find that other things work better, we'll try them. All we need is an efficient method.'

It is true that we need an efficient method; but we also have to think of the effects on the pupil in terms of his general attitude to, and grasp of, rules, because what we do with this task ('law and order') will obviously affect the amount of difficulty we have with the other ('educational') task that we have just discussed. We need a method that is efficient *and* gives the pupil a clear idea of what a rule is (even if, in this case, we are not too much concerned with the reasons he has for obeying it). It is very difficult to get completely away from what goes on in the pupil's head; we can say, 'So long as the rules are kept, for this purpose it doesn't matter why they're kept', but do we really mean this? Suppose you could ensure that all the rules were kept by hypnotizing the pupils, so that they 'obeyed the rules' like sleep-walkers; certainly, there would be 'law and order' and no trouble, but if the pupils were really in a trance, they could hardly be said to be 'obeying the rules' in the full sense (any more than a child tied up in a straitjacket is really 'well-behaved').

So even as regards this task we want the pupils to be conscious, to obey the rules for some sort of reason. Now the reason that is, in a sense, nearest to a proper understanding of what rules are turns out also to operate as a very efficient method for getting the rules kept. We refer to the operation of sanctions or punishments. Some people dislike the whole idea of punishment, but it is easy to see that it is inevitable: what makes something a rule (rather than just a pious hope, or a wish, or an ideal) is that it is backed by some form of sanction or punishment. Societies and institutions have got to have rules, and rules (to be rules) must have sanctions attached to them. (These sanctions or punishments may be of very different kinds: whether we should use corporal punishment, or keep pupils in after school, or frown at them, or send them out of the room —

that is, what *form* the punishment should take — is another matter.)

Punishment is a necessary part of the notion of a rule, and it is also the most obvious (we do not say the best) reason for keeping a rule — that is, punishment is quite closely connected with a rule's being a rule (rather than just something the teacher hopes the pupil will do). It has, of course, to be unpleasant, otherwise it would not be punishment, and it has to follow, always or usually, when and because a rule has been broken (otherwise it is not a rule). Somebody who gives up the idea of punishment has given up the idea of having rules, and somebody who does not have clear and clearly-enforced punishments does not have clear and clearly-enforced rules. If you do not have clear and clearly-enforced rules, two disastrous things follow. First, the institution (school) is chaotic. Teachers wear themselves out trying to make up for the chaos by being 'interesting', or working harder, or cajoling, or persuading, but these expedients are poor substitutes for a clear and clearly enforced set of rules (see chapter 8). Secondly, the pupils have no chance at all of being educated in respect of rules and discipline (our second task), since they are not presented with them properly. We are tempted to say that many (even most) schools do not have rules that are clear or clearly enforced. There are lots of reasons for this, and teachers are not the only ones to blame, but it needs putting right (see Wilson, 1981).

For our first task, 'law and order', we should use the sanctions or punishments that are attached to (in a sense, *part* of) the rules in order to get the obedience we want. This means, of course, that the sanctions have to be not only clear but also sufficient: that is, strong enough to ensure that the rules are obeyed. This, again, is in strong contrast with any other (irrelevant) reasons for obedience — for instance, the teacher's personality. The sanctions must be presented, on the contrary, as impersonally as possible — more as if the class were playing a game: if you commit a foul, there is a prescribed penalty. There should not be any question of teachers persuading, or getting angry, or being strict or lenient or 'democratic' or 'authoritarian': all these lead the pupils away from the idea of obeying a rule.

This impersonality will make it much easier when it comes to the second task, that of improving a pupil's reasons for obedience. For now he will be less tempted to see rules as personal edicts —

what Mr So-and-so insists on, or what 'they' (the 'authorities', whom he perhaps hates) make 'us' (the underdogs) do. We can attach the notion of a rule not to individual people but to the job that the rule does — maintaining order, making it easier for people to be educated. Rules are not commands or requests by individuals. And, obviously, in improving pupils' reasons for obedience, we can help them to understand by letting them make up their own rules, or see what happens if they do not have any, or try out different ones. But all this means that we, as teachers, have to be very clear about rules, and the reasons for them, in the first place.

Discipline, then, consists in obedience — for the right sort of reasons — to rules set up by an accepted authority. We have seen that it is absurd (indeed, impossible) to get rid of the whole apparatus of rules/authority/sanctions, but we have not said very much about the kind of rules or the kind of authority that teachers should enforce. Is there anything that we can say about this? Well, we have already said that the point of rules is to get a particular job (in our case, education) done efficiently, and that the teacher must have (as, at least in theory, he does have) the authority to get the rules obeyed. But this leaves the teacher a good deal of latitude. Is he to run the kind of rule-governed system that a dictator, for instance, might run? Or should he be willing to share some of his authority with the pupils? And would he be wise to impose the same rules and punishments on all pupils at all times? In fact, as we know, different teachers and schools run very different systems. Now, is this just a question of finding out (perhaps from psychologists or sociologists) what works best, or are there any general principles involved that we need to understand before-hand?

We think there are, chiefly because of the point we made earlier about the teacher's educational task. We saw that, in considering how to achieve 'law and order', we cannot be concerned only with what sanctions or punishments are efficient because the kind of sanctions we use will affect the pupils' whole view and understanding of rules and discipline. We must have sanctions that are efficient and help (or anyway do not hinder) the pupils' understanding. The same goes for the question of what rules and systems we should operate. Obviously, we want those that are best educationally or help to get education done, as we have said. But there will be two aspects to this question. First, we want rules and systems that make it easier for us to get the *rest of* 'education' done properly — that ensure, for instance, that the pupils are reasonably well-behaved and attentive and that they do not interfere with each other and so on, so that they can learn their mathematics and English and other subjects properly. But, second, we want rules and systems that help to educate the pupils *in respect of their understanding of rules and systems.* This is a different objective and may sometimes conflict with the first.

A parallel may make this a bit clearer. Suppose I am a benevolent dictator or government ruling a backward or primitive people. Then I have one objective, to operate rules and systems that will in general be best for my people; and these might be pretty simple and 'undemocratic', since things may work best if they simply obey me like young children. So I make and hand out laws that they obey unthinkingly, and everything goes well: the railways run on time, chaos is avoided, and so on. But I may also have another objective, which is to educate the people so that they can eventually come to govern themselves; and they will not be able to do this without some understanding and experience of rules and systems. In order to promote these, I sometimes let them make up their own rules (even if they are obviously silly), and I give them practice in different sorts of systems, and discuss the whole issue with them and so on. And this objective may sometimes conflict with the first.

Teachers have to be concerned with both objectives. What we want to know from psychologists and others is what rules and systems fit different types of pupil — obviously there will be considerable variation depending on the pupils' age, intelligence, home background, etc. — from the viewpoint of the smooth running of things. For instance, maybe young children need clearer and simpler rules than older ones (or maybe not — this is the sort of thing we have to find out). But we also want to know what sorts of experience of rules and systems give different types of pupil the best *understanding* of rules and systems in general. These aims may conflict; we may have to give up some of our smooth running in order to promote in our pupils an understanding of rules and systems.

The point to remember throughout all this is that there is no one set of rules or system that is always right. It is silly to discuss whether teachers should be 'democratic' or 'authoritarian' or 'liberal' or 'traditional' (or whatever jargon may be used) because, very obviously, teachers need to operate different systems at different times, depending on the context. Sometimes (as in our sailing-ship example) pupils need to get used to an order-and-obedience context, in which there is no question of discussion or argument: sometimes (as in a seminar discussion) they need to get used to a context in which everyone operates on a more equal footing. What is important is to look at the whole range of possible contexts, each of which has its own appropriate set of rules. Sometimes the teacher will want discussion and intervention by the children; sometimes he needs complete silence and attention. Sometimes the pupils should obey his orders instantly; at other times it may be a good idea for them to make up their own rules.

The other really important thing is to be clear, and *to make it clear to the pupils,* what system is operating at any one time — and, of course, to retain the ultimate authority and discipline that are necessary in any system. Thus there will be occasions on which the teacher may want to say, 'Right, for the next hour you're going to do so-and-so (a classroom project, or something outside the school, or anything). I'm not going to tell you how to do it. Appoint your own leaders if you want to, make your own rules, and do it, and then we'll talk about it.' The teacher has to enforce or organize this ('democratic') context just like any other context. Behind all the experiences he wants to give the pupils there must be his authority as an educator, and this means that he must make the rules absolutely clear to the pupils, particularly when he wants to try out a different system for a particular purpose. If he does not, they will easily get muddled because they will probably be used to one general system; new systems will have to be spelled out to them very carefully.

One could perhaps describe this as a kind of political education. It is obviously of great practical importance for pupils' whole attitudes to 'authority', 'morality', 'values', and that whole area of life. There is a lot to be found out by experience, research and trial and error in this field, but a teacher who has the main points and objectives clear, and who knows his pupils, will not go far wrong.

5

Teaching a Subject

A lot of teachers think something like this: 'My subject is mathematics (or English, or geography, or whatever). Certainly, there's a lot of argument about how to teach mathematics — whether children should be taught to recite the multiplication tables, whether we should introduce them to other systems besides the decimal system and so on. But at least I know what mathematics is: after all, I've spent a long time learning it myself. And at least I know what it is to teach mathematics, even if I'm not sure what the best methods are: after all, I've spent a long time teaching it. So isn't it silly to ask general questions about subjects, since we know the answers already?'

But if we think a bit harder, we may not feel quite as sure of ourselves. With mathematics and some other subjects (we shall come back to these later) it seems reasonable to say that we do know at least what the subjects are. But do we know this with subjects called, say, 'R. E.', or 'social studies', or perhaps even 'English'? We may not feel as sure of the content of these subjects. We may want to ask, 'Just what are we supposed to be doing or trying to do under these headings? Just what is it to teach R. E. or social studies?' And it is important — perhaps also rather alarming — that we are not entirely clear about the answer. For how can we teach these subjects well, or indeed at all, if we do not first know what they are?

If we are to get any further with this question, we have to be clear that we are not asking two other questions. Suppose I am fairly confident that I know what mathematics is, what it is to

teach mathematics. Then I can go on to ask about the best
methods of teaching it (and discuss whether to make young children
learn their tables, etc.), and about the point or aims of teaching it
(how useful it is in the modern world? Does it improve children's
thinking generally?). These two questions are different, of course,
but they are both also quite different from the issue of what it is to
teach X.

It is important to see that we have to start with this issue, for
how can we sensibly discuss the best methods of teaching something
or the general point of teaching it if we do not know what it is?
Suppose we thought about going on a course about the aims and
methods of teaching squiggleology. Well, unless we were pretty
clear about what squiggleology was, about what content was
covered by the word, we would not know how to start talking
about how to teach it or about what point there was in teaching it.
Now, we are a bit clearer about what some subjects (like
mathematics) are than about what squiggleology is but not always
much clearer, although sometimes we think we are. A lot of talk
about the 'aims and methods of teaching X' (say, English, or
history, or perhaps even mathematics) may be muddled or a waste
of time just because we are not, in fact, as clear about what X is as
we like to think.

To put this another way: in a conference about (say) 'teaching
English' or 'teaching classics', different people may have quite
different ideas about what 'English' or 'classics' is. To one person,
perhaps, 'English' means lots of grammar and parsing and neatly
written exercises and so on: to another, it means impromptu
drama and reading some 'socially relevant' novels with the pupils.
Similarly, one man's idea of 'classics' may be learning irregular
verbs and construing Caesar; another's may be to give the pupils
some idea of what the Greeks and Romans were like, to take them
on visits to Roman buildings and so on. Unless we reach some
agreement about what we mean by 'English' or 'classics', any
discussion on the 'aims and methods' of teaching them will be at
cross-purposes.

We all need to hang on to this point tightly because otherwise
we are very apt to go off the rails in a certain way that we will try to
illustrate. Suppose I am paid to teach music, and I find myself
working in a society (perhaps some Communist country) where
people are very politically minded. They tell me I should not

introduce the children to Beethoven 'because he was a middle-
class bourgeois', or that it is wrong for pupils to like Strauss
'because he supported the Nazis'. Now, if I am not careful, I may
find myself arguing politics with the authorities. I might say,
'There's nothing wrong with being middle-class', or 'Anyone might
have made the same mistake as Strauss', or something like that.
But what I ought to say is, 'My job is to teach music, not politics:
teaching music doesn't have anything to do with politics. It doesn't
matter, for anyone interested in music, what Beethoven's or
Strauss's political views were. If their political or social views
really do help us to understand and appreciate their music, they
might be worth mentioning, but otherwise not.'

Most of us would probably think that in such cases politics or
other marginal considerations are *obviously* irrelevant. But now
consider 'teaching English'. Suppose the people around me are
very keen that children should learn to love their neighbours, or be
good citizens, or get on well with their friends. They may want me
to gear my English teaching to these aims and may put pressure on
me to make the pupils read certain books (the ones they think will
increase the pupils' 'concern' or 'citizenship') and not others. This
is just like the music and politics case, even though here we may
have more sympathy with the aims. What we ought to say is, 'No
doubt your aims — loving one's neighbour and so on — are very
desirable, but that isn't part of what we mean by 'teaching English'.
My English teaching may or may not make better or more loving
citizens. It may also make the children happier or less happy, more
or less able to 'think critically' or 'be creative'. It may have all sorts
of 'spin-offs'. But these don't count as *what it is to teach English*.
Some of them may perhaps count as part of what is meant by, say,
'moral education' or 'civics' but not 'English'.'

What happens here is that we get carried away by some external
aim, some kind of benefit we want to bestow on our pupils.
Perhaps we want them to have the right kind of politics or morality,
or not to be indoctrinated with 'middle-class values', or to be
happy and socially confident, or 'creative', or 'critical', or
'autonomous'. We call these 'external' aims because (however
desirable they may be) they do not count as aims inside the
subject. Another example: it may be true, in general, that learning
history makes people less prejudiced about other people and races
and that it gives them more insight into 'current affairs' — and no

doubt these are desirable outcomes. But 'learning history' does not *mean* becoming less prejudiced or better at 'current affairs', as is obvious from the fact that there are people who are good at history or know a lot of history but are still prejudiced and ignorant about all sorts of things. The 'internal' aims of learning history — what counts as 'learning history' — have no necessary connection with this 'external' aim.

It is no good being carried away like this, however important the 'external' aims are. For although we may indeed say things like, 'Teaching history (English, etc.) is important because it makes pupils into better citizens and happier people, and this is a crying need, so let's get on with it', we cannot easily know whether this is true; not because we have not done enough research into whether historians make better citizens, but because we have not a clear idea of what 'teaching history' is, so how can we say whether it makes better citizens or not? It is like saying, 'Teaching squiggleology makes happier pupils': it would be no good replying, 'Yes, it does' or 'No, it doesn't' — we should have to start by getting clear what squiggleology was.

The only way out of this is a way that we do not think anyone, on reflection, would actually want to take: that is, to get rid of the whole idea of 'subjects' altogether. But we can see the temptation. We may think that a child's happiness, or politics, or self-confidence is so important that we should not waste our time on school subjects, and start calling these 'academic' or 'unreal' or 'irrelevant'. So we abolish all subject titles like 'mathematics', 'English', 'history', 'French' and so on (or perhaps we keep one or two extremely vague ones, like 'the environment' or 'society'), and then we find it hard even to ask (let alone answer) questions about what it is to teach any subject.

There are various reasons why this way out is not possible, but it is important first to see that the reason is not that the 'external' aims might be thought unimportant. We are not saying, 'It doesn't matter whether children are happy, "creative", "aware", etc.: they must be made to get on with serious academic work.' The reasons lie deeper. If we are going to do anything we could seriously call educating children (rather than just being nice to them), we will be concerned that they should have some kind of knowledge, or abilities, or skills, or types of competence. But — this is the point — we cannot give them knowledge or competence in general: it is bound to be knowledge *of* something or competence *at* something; it is bound to be some kind, or different kinds, of knowledge and competence. For instance, a child can learn to play football and/or chess and/or badminton; but he cannot learn to play them all at the same time, just because they are different games. Similarly, you can teach a child about animals and plants or about geology and rock formations, or introduce him to the beauties of the countryside, but you cannot do all these at exactly the same time because they are different kinds of knowledge and experience. You might or might not want to bring them all under one subject title, like perhaps 'nature study' or 'the natural environment', but they would still be different.

This difference is a matter of logic and has nothing to do with wanting to 'break down subject barriers' or any other modern educational idea. It just is the case — it could not be otherwise, whatever you did — that some kinds of interests and questions are different from others. Being interested in why birds migrate is different from being interested in how rocks are formed, and still more different from being interested in what makes a beautiful landscape or what sort of houses would spoil it. Asking about how Hitler rose to power is different from asking whether the word 'Hitler' means anything and different from asking about whether Hitler was a good man. Of course, there may be connections between these interests, but they are still different.

These differences are what make 'subjects' inevitable. Suppose you take some children to see a church. Sooner or later, whatever your views about 'subjects', they are going to be interested in it in different ways. Some children will be interested in how it is built or how the spire manages to stay up when it is so tall — that is the start of 'mechanics' or part of 'architecture'. Other children will be interested in who built it and why, how it got to be there, and who wanted it — the start of 'history'. Others may want to know what it is for and what goes on in it — 'religion' or perhaps 'sociology'. And so on. It is inevitable that you should cater for these different interests in different ways simply because they *are* different. If a child asks, 'How does the spire manage to stand up, miss?' and you reply, 'Yes, isn't it beautiful? It cost £5000 and was built in 1876', you will not be able to educate him at all; what he wants to know, now anyway, is something about stresses and structures and building.

So we have to make 'subjects' fit different interests. This is a long and difficult business because many subjects have grown up in a rather haphazard way, not necessarily because of the differences in the particular angles from which people might be interested in things but for quite other reasons. Some of the reasons have to do with our history: for instance, when science became important we began to do less Latin, Greek and theology and more biology, physics and mathematics. Other subjects are studied as a result of tradition or inertia. This gives us a very mixed bag of subject titles. But what we have to do is not to try to scrap the lot but to look much more closely and carefully at all of them, so that we can find out what we are trying to do. Before we start some major operation that we might call 'changing the curriculum', we have to be clear about what we are doing now, and this brings us inevitably back to questions like 'What is it to teach such-and-such?'

Now, when we stop to think, we know quite well — or if we do not, Professor Hirst has told us (Hirst and Peters, 1970) — that subject titles can be of two kinds. First, we can be interested in, and study, some things or phenomena: we may want to know about trees, or motor cars, or what grandfather did when he was a little boy. Subject titles such as 'the motor car', or 'forestry', or 'race prejudice' are like this. Second, we can be interested in looking at lots of things from specific *angles* or by means of specific *disciplines*: for instance, we may be interested in the general business of why things work, in making observations and doing experiments on all sorts of things in the physical world, not anything in particular — in this case, we might call our subject 'science' or 'scientific method'.

It is important to see how different these are. A person's attention might be captured by certain things — say, churches. He just likes them or is fascinated by them in a general sort of way. He likes learning anything to do with them — the history of churches, their architecture, how they are decorated, who goes to them and so on — and he might not be interested in other buildings, such as town halls or palaces. Another person is interested less in things than in a particular angle or approach to them. He is interested, say, in architecture — not just church architecture but the architecture of all sorts of buildings. His attachment is to a particular discipline.

When we ask of any subject 'What is it to teach such-and-such?', we have to bear this difference very much in mind, otherwise we may be misled by the subject title. For instance, a pupil who is keen on learning about battles in the Napoleonic Wars might be said to be 'interested in history'. And he is indeed interested in some of the *phenomena* that we deal with under the title 'history', namely, the battles. We might say he is interested in the history (or some aspects of the history) of the Napoleonic Wars. But is he also interested in 'history' as a discipline, or is he just interested in battles? To be interested in history as a discipline means to like, in general, to find out things about the past doings of men. Again, to be interested in 'science' ('scientific method') means to be keen on finding out why things happen as they do in the physical world.

So the first thing we have to decide about any subject title, if we ask 'What is it to teach X?', is whether X is to be the name of a thing or set of phenomena, or the name of a discipline or angle or approach. Sometimes the answer to this is pretty clear. 'Mathematics' or 'logic', for instance, do not name things. Certainly, we could say that mathematics was 'about numbers and figures and so on' or that logic was 'about statements and truth', but more naturally we would say that to learn mathematics was to learn a particular kind of thinking, a set of techniques, a discipline. 'A good mathematician' is somebody who is good at this kind of thinking. Equally obviously, titles like 'the motor car' or 'race prejudice' stand not for particular disciplines but for particular things or phenomena — that is, for motor cars and race prejudice.

But other cases need more thought. 'English' (like 'French' and other titles of the study of languages) seems to refer to certain phenomena; but a title like 'literary criticism' or 'literary appreciation' obviously refers to a kind of discipline, a particular style of thought (which one might use on other literature besides English). 'Science' seems to refer to a discipline, but when we talk of 'biology', 'zoology', 'physics', etc., we indicate that we are using the discipline in a limited way, applying it only to certain things or phenomena and not to others. ('Zoology', for example, is the discipline of science as applied only to living things.) 'History' might be taken to be a discipline, but a course or subject called 'the history of the French Revolution', though it would obviously have to use the discipline of 'history', would refer specifically to a limited range of phenomena — that is, what happened in the French Revolution. Finally, we have to note that quite a few titles

— 'classics', 'social studies', 'R. E.', 'moral education' and plenty of others — are so imprecise that the actual words may not be much of a guide. In some cases it may be more a matter of deciding *what we are going to mean by* (say) 'classics', than of deciding what we *do in fact mean* by it; for there may not be anything very specific which we do mean.

Observe now — this is pretty obvious — that even when the subject title is the name of a thing (rather than a discipline), you still have to use some discipline in order to study the thing. For instance, 'the motor car' is a 'thing' title, but it is not possible to be interested in motor cars except by being interested in various aspects of them (perhaps in all aspects). At any one time you will be asking questions about one of these different aspects — for instance, about their development over the last fifty years (that is history), or about how they work (that is science), or about their appearance and whether they look nice (that is art appreciation or 'aesthetics'). So — as we saw in the case of pupils who were interested in churches — we cannot avoid having subjects in the sense of 'disciplines', whatever we do with the subject titles. Thus if we decided to 'get rid of subjects' altogether and wiped all the subject-titles off the notice board (or replaced them all with a single title like 'life' or 'the world'), we would still have to be clear about what we were doing in any single classroom period, or for the next ten minutes, or for any particular time-span.

So it would obviously be useful to compile a list of the disciplines: that is, a list of the various angles from which pupils can be interested in things, of the kinds of questions and answers and knowledge that apply to different aspects of them. This is not easy because it is not easy to know just how to chop up different kinds of human knowledge and experience. But certainly one of the more promising lists has been made by Hirst (Hirst and Peters (1970)), and it is worth looking at it to see how the disciplines or 'forms of thought' (as he calls them) might relate to subject titles as they appear in school curricula.

Logic/mathematics This kind of knowledge is not about the world of our sense experience at all but about logical derivations from certain rules or axioms. In some ways, it is like playing a game. You start with the axioms of Euclid or rules about the meaning of certain signs and symbols, and then you derive further knowledge from these. We all have a fairly clear idea what sort of operation this is, and the school subjects that come under the general title 'mathematics' are clear examples of it.

Science This kind of knowledge is about the physical world, about causes and effects in nature: why things fall downwards, why planets move in ellipses and so on. Again, this is pretty clear, and we can identify this discipline in subjects entitled 'chemistry', or 'physics', or 'biology'.

Personal knowledge This is more difficult. But you can see that when we ask questions about why *people* do things (not why planets or light waves do things), it is a different sort of study. People have intentions, purposes and plans, which planets do not have. So 'Why did he . . .?' means something very different from 'Why did it . . .?' And, as we would expect, the sort of evidence with which we need to work is different: for people we need evidence about what goes on in their heads — about their intentions and designs. The clearest case of a subject title that uses this discipline is 'history', which is surely about why people did things in the past. (If we were interested in why eclipses or earthquakes happened in the past, that would be more like science.) Some aspects of what goes on under titles like 'psychology' or 'sociology' may be also concerned with personal knowledge, though other aspects may be more like science: it all depends what sort of answers and knowledge we are after.

Morality, aesthetics and religion These are more difficult still. We lump them together partly because it is not clear what ground each of the three words covers, and there may be some overlap. (Thus for some people 'morality' is part of 'religion', or at least importantly connected with it.) But it seems plausible to say that there are questions about what is morally right and wrong, which are different from questions about what is beautiful, or ugly, or dainty, or elegant ('aesthetics'), and perhaps different again from questions about what one should worship or pray to ('religion'). Philosophers have been working on these areas, trying to help us get clearer about them, but even now we can see that some subject-titles include some of these disciplines. Thus if under the title of 'English' I try to get children to appreciate the elegance or effectiveness of a poem or a play, that looks like 'aesthetics' — and it is similar to (the same sort of discipline as) what the French teacher might do with a French poem or what the music teacher might do in musical appreciation classes.

It is worth noting here, incidentally, that not being as clear as we ought to be about these disciplines holds up all possible progress in some cases. The most obvious example is R. E. We have the subject title 'R. E.' (or 'R. I.' or 'scripture' or 'divinity' or anything we like to choose), but it does not help unless we know what *sort* of knowledge — what discipline — is involved in teaching R. E.. We can sidestep the problem by, say, teaching church history in R. E. periods, but that is the discipline of history or personal knowledge and might well be left to the history teachers; or we can encourage children to appreciate the beauty of biblical language, but that is the discipline of aesthetics or literary appreciation and might well be left to the English teacher. Religious people at least will feel that there is something missing if that is all we do. The problem for such people is to point out a special kind of discipline, with a special kind of knowledge, that should go on under 'R. E.'.

This kind of list is very useful to bear in mind when we are considering rather vaguely entitled new subjects, as perhaps 'social studies' or 'the environment' or 'sex education'. For we at once want to know what disciplines are going to be involved, and the list allows us to raise the question against a useful background. Is 'sex education', for instance, going to be just science (teaching about biology and contraception and so on)? Or are we going to bring in personal knowledge also (helping pupils to understand their own and other people's feelings)? And are we going to raise questions about what is right and wrong (morality)? These can all be seen as different issues. Until we are clear about which disciplines we are going to bring in, these subject-titles will be hopelessly vague.

It is remarkable how many subject-titles there are in school curricula that do not fit neatly into any single discipline. Mathematics, the sciences and perhaps history fit clearly enough into identifiable categories, but consider again titles like 'English', 'classics', 'geography', 'French' and so on. It seems pretty clear that these subjects involve a number of different disciplines. Sometimes it is also clear what the disciplines are: 'geography', for instance, is 'science' in so far as we ask questions about the physical world ('physical geography') and 'personal knowledge' when we ask about why people do things ('human geography'). But often even this is not very clear. Try working out what disciplines might be involved in 'English', 'French', 'classics' or, indeed, in learning to read and write. It is not as easy.

Fortunately, there are other ways in which we can get clearer about 'what it is to teach such-and-such'. One way is to take a closer look at the particular body of knowledge or set of abilities that is normally associated with the subject title. It is important to realize here that though some subject-titles are vaguer than others, normally not just anything counts as 'teaching such-and-such'. (You might get away with almost anything under an extremely vague title like 'the environment' but not with more usual titles like 'English' or 'French'.) Thus we would not normally talk of someone being good at English or knowing a lot about English if he could not spell simple English words, or could not write clear English sentences or had not ever heard of Shakespeare or Dickens; these seem pretty central to the idea of 'English', and we can say this even though we may not be completely clear about exactly what disciplines, from Hirst's list or from any other logical list of the kind, are involved.

We are suggesting, then, that the best starting-point for teachers who want to be clear about what it is to teach a particular subject is to take the subject-title seriously. If you start in this way, it gradually becomes clear which different kinds of knowledge and abilities are involved — what the differences between them are — and then we can give them more appropriate titles, if these do not already exist. In doing this, you have to compare what the subject-title suggests with what does (or might) actually go in in school periods; often this has alarming results, as in the case of 'R. E.'. (If in an R. E. period a teacher discussed the problems of homeless people, or sex, or the language of the Psalms, we should want to ask, 'But can we fairly describe that as education in *religion?*' The title 'R. E.' does not match up to what is actually discussed in the period.)

Teachers of various subjects must do this job of sorting out titles and practices for themselves (it would take far too long here), but we will take one example to make the task clearer. Suppose we have 'French' on the timetable. We look round at what happens in schools and find that different people do different things: (a) get the pupils to speak and understand ordinary French orally (perhaps in a language laboratory or by sending them to French families); (b) get them to read and write French correctly; (c) acquaint them with the classics of French literature (Racine and Molière and so on); (d) explain to them how modern French grew out of Latin, via medieval French; (e) familiarize them with the French way of life and the countryside of France; (f) explain to them various aspects of French history, politics and geography; (g) try to make them less prejudiced about the French people and more in favour of the Common Market; (h) take them for a canoe trip down the Rhône; (i) give them a good time in Paris for a weekend.

We need to start by asking, 'Which of these count as "learning French"?' We would accept (a) and (b) without much hesitation and perhaps classify them more clearly under 'the French language'. If we wanted to bring in (c), we should have to make this clear by saying 'French literature' (you can 'know French' without knowing anything about French literature). With (d) we might hesitate a bit: it is not 'learning French' exactly, but it gives pupils a better and fuller understanding of why modern French is as it is: perhaps we can classify it under 'the French language'. With (e) and (f) we should hesitate a good deal more: these things might sometimes be relevant to 'learning French' (for instance, you might have to see the Normandy countryside to understand properly what *bocage* means) but perhaps not very often. They are really more like (g), which is really concerned not with 'learning French' at all but rather with moral education or the education of the emotions, or perhaps politics or economics. (h) and (i), again, are not part of what is meant by 'learning French' — they may (or may not) be good ways of getting pupils interested in 'learning French', but that is different. (And this is a very important difference: teachers may have to do all sorts of things to get their pupils interested in a subject, but that is not the same as actually teaching it.)

In this example we have roughly sorted out nine activities, (a) to (i), that are candidates for part of what is meant, or might be meant, by 'learning French'. We have left out all sorts of other candidates, and we have separated them or sorted them far too casually and roughly; but it is very important that we start in this way because what we need first (in the case of any subject title) is a clear list of different things that are not aims of 'teaching French' but part of what it is to teach French or what might be thought to be part of it. It is only too easy to avoid this task and to try to produce lists of objectives in a high-minded and muddled way. And this leads to chaos. For instance, we might compile a list of objectives that included these items: to assist the pupils' understanding of French culture and literature; to familiarize the pupils with French thought and life; to give them a sound working knowledge of the language and thereby to improve their self-expression and ability to communicate with others; to acquaint them with the best and most profound writings in French, both past and present; and so on. You can see how useless this exercise is. First, half the time this list has its eye on 'external' aims (e.g. 'to improve their self-expression') and not on what it is to teach French. But worse, the items on the list overlap hopelessly. If we 'familiarize the pupils with French thought', do not we thereby 'assist the pupils' understanding of French culture and literature'? And is not that also partly the same as acquainting them 'with the best and most profound writings in French'? Unless the items on such lists are discrete — that is, logically distinct and separate from each other — the lists are useless.

Of course, items (a) to (i) on our list are only a start, but at least they are different, and at least we can start to form some fairly clear concept of what falls within the notion 'teaching French' and what does not. Thus we allow, let us suppose, (a), (b), (c) and (d), but not the rest. We could in principle run the same sort of operation for 'teaching English', 'mathematics' and anything else — though in some cases, like perhaps 'classics', the title would be so vague that we might be in more doubt. (Yet even here we have some idea of what counts: if a teacher spent his time telling pupils about classic race meetings or films shown at the Classic Cinema, we should say either that he was a rogue or that he did not know what 'classics' meant in education.)

Now this is a start, but of course it does not solve all our curricular problems (though it may in itself help teachers to be clear about their own subjects at least). For now we think, 'Very well, we have a clearer idea of what's meant by "teaching X". But do the things that fall *outside* that concept — (e), (f), (g) and so on — have to be written off? Might not they be very important? Ought not they to be catered for somehow?' This thought is quite right. But the point is that as a result of making such a list and seeing the differences and distinctions between the very various

things that we can do with pupils, we begin to see more clearly
what sort of thing each is, and perhaps how in principle we might
cater for it (not necessarily in French lessons).

Take (e), for instance — the item about familiarizing pupils with
the French countryside. This may be important, but would not it
be better done under the heading of 'geography'? Or (g), trying to
diminish their prejudice: if we are serious about wanting to diminish
racial prejudice, why on earth should we try to do this under the
heading of 'learning French'? Why not get down to the job of
trying to determine what produces or diminishes racial prejudice
and have special periods about it — or perhaps not periods at all,
but some other approach altogether (role-playing, or visits to
French families)? Or (i), the Paris weekend: if our idea is to give
pupils a good time — and why not, every now and then? — that is
fair enough, but there might be a cheaper and better way.

If we look at these differences and distinctions hard enough, we
shall begin to make sense of how to cater for our aims, and this is
of practical value in two ways. First, we cater for them more
effectively by understanding them and giving them importance in
their own right; and, second, we avoid messing up existing subjects
by bringing in irrelevant and extraneous issues. For instance,
suppose we are looking at 'English' or 'English literature'. One of
the things that might emerge, if we made a list, could be something
like 'getting the pupils to understand and sympathize with other
people'. A very worthy aim, but not obviously central to the notion
of 'teaching English'. This fits better under some title like 'moral
education'. If we do not fit it in there, where it belongs, two bad
things happen. First, we do not cater properly for moral education
but just vaguely hope it happens in 'English' periods; and, second,
we do not concentrate properly on 'teaching English' because we
vaguely feel we have to do moral education as well in those
periods. This is a muddle and does nobody any good.

The task is obviously a vast and complex one and not necessarily
to be undertaken by particular subject teachers (though they can
help with it). Let us assume that, some of the time, we are getting
on with the task — that is, trying to get clear about, and cater
for things that *do not* count as 'teaching X' itself: then there
are still some other considerations to be remembered, not yet
mentioned. We still do not mean considerations of 'method'
(or of 'aims'): we mean considerations about what it is to

teach (or learn) X. There are two in particular.

First, it is not always as easy as we have made it sound to say what counts as X and what does not. We have to keep X separated from other subjects or disciplines — as when we say, 'But surely that's really geography,' or 'That's not really English; it's moral education.' But we also have to keep X separated from very general sorts of knowledge, or abilities, or character traits. For instance, if a pupil has a speech impediment and finds difficulty in talking, the French (or English) teacher might try to cope with this by teaching the child to speak French (or English). Certainly, being able to speak French involves being able to speak in general, but this general ability is not part of learning French as such.

To take a more difficult example, suppose we have a title like 'mathematics'. Now, when we teach children about fractions or multiplication or decimals we have no doubt that these are 'mathematics'. But suppose we have a child who does not see that if A is bigger than B and B is bigger than C, then A is bigger than C, or a child who seems to think that somehow there is 'more' water when you pour it from a short fat vessel into a tall thin one, as in Piaget's experiments. We are dealing here with very general notions about space and volume and logic — do these really come under 'mathematics'? This would be like saying that teaching a child what 'yesterday' means comes under 'history'.

There are lots of questions of this kind (and no single, simple answers to them.) All we are doing here is to point to the difficulty of determining the cut-off point (so to speak) at which we are going to say, 'That's not teaching such-and-such specifically; that's trying to give the child more intelligence, or certain very general concepts which he needs for any subject, or the ability to concentrate in general.' There must be such cut-off points, otherwise we can fix no clear idea of any subject as such at all. A subject-teacher needs a clear idea of what being able to learn his subject presupposes, if only in order to distinguish that from what learning his subject consists of. This has to be worked out in each case.

Second, a different kind of consideration, but one that is of immense importance for practical teaching: even assuming that we are quite clear about the boundary lines of a subject, we can still emphasize certain aspects at the expense of others. We do not mean by 'aspects' different parts of the subject — for instance, spelling as against oral communication in English, or algebra rather than geometry in mathematics. We are referring, rather, to the different kinds of interest a pupil or teacher might have in a subject or (better) the different ways in which they might see the subject.

This is not easy to explain, though we all have a fairly clear idea of it in a way. For example, one mathematics teacher may be comparatively uninterested in whether pupils really understand the basic logic and concepts behind various operations, such as multiplying fractions and solving equations, and is worried only about whether they can actually conduct the operations — whether they can multiply fractions and solve equations. Such a man might say, 'Never mind why x squared minus y squared can be written $(x - y)(x + y)$, just do it.' Another teacher may not mind so much about what the pupils can do — whether they can do long division and remember formulae for working out areas — as long as they really have a grasp of the concepts involved.

Again, one Latin teacher may just present his class with the words *Arma virumque cano* and say, 'That means "I sing of arms and the man"', without worrying about the grammar and construction. Another might say, '*Arma* is in the accusative, object of *cano : vir* means "a man" as opposed to a woman, here perhaps something more like "a hero"', and so on. The first wants to get on with it, so to speak — he is interested in getting the pupils to grasp the general flow of meaning — whereas the second wants to make sure that they really know how the language works. (We might say the first is more interested in getting across what Virgil is saying; the second is more interested in *Latin.*) Or a French teacher might say, 'Never mind about the grammar of what you're saying. Just make the noises of *Merci mille fois, monsieur.*' Or a history teacher might say, 'The Normans invaded in 1066 and their duke became the first English king. . . . No, never mind for the moment who the Normans were, children, or why they were called Normans, or exactly what a duke is (he's a sort of leader). Let's get on with what happened.' Other French and history teachers might prefer to stop and work out things in more detail before going on.

We want to make it clear, again, that we are not talking about the best method of teaching children the same content, but really about different contents. Thus I might learn everything about chess either by having all the moves and pieces explained to me first and then playing, or by starting to play much sooner and picking up the moves and other details as I play. Which method suits me best is a matter of technique (and/or my own temperament). But with subjects it can be different. One person, for instance, may be very good at doing things in mathematics (mental arithmetic, solving equations, etc.) but without much grasp of the logic of the operations; another may understand all about set theory and the basic axioms of mathematics but be hopeless at performing with them because he has not been given the teaching or the practice. One person may be able to give a reasonable account of what Virgil's *Aeneid* is about but be quite unable to construe one line of it; another may be good at working out just how the words fit but not know much about the poem as a whole.

Again, there is no single 'answer' to this — that is, no question of its always being right to 'get on with it' or always being right to understand everything first. This would lead to absurdity. To understand *everything* about the words *Arma virumque cano,* we should have to go into why these words had the form they did in classical Latin, all the various meanings of *vir* (with parallels from other authors), the basic roots and derivations of the words and so on, just as to understand everything in even the simplest mathematics operation would, strictly speaking, take us right back to the logical foundations or philosophy of mathematics (the axioms of Peano or Russell's and Whitehead's *Principia Mathematica*). On the other hand, without some understanding we should have nothing but parroted learning — the pupils would not really acquire any knowledge at all, except knowledge of how to make appropriate noises.

This sort of dimension runs through all subjects: it is difficult, and may be misleading, to describe the opposite ends of it at all, but we might briefly call one end 'wanting to get to the roots of it' and the other end 'wanting to get on with it'. It is likely that nearly all children have both desires in them, and certainly all subjects include both these aspects. For the practising teacher it is a matter of how far he wants to go along this dimension in either direction. One way is not necessarily better than the other, but it can be very different. Thus there is a lot of difference between someone who can speak good French but has never thought, or been taught, about why some words are right in some places and others wrong, and someone who can give a good account of French grammar and syntax but is bad at speaking; or between the person who knows about Latin culture and poetry but does not know much Latin. These differences can be (as here) so big that they virtually break the subject down into two separate topics.

All we can do here — but it is important to do it — is to get these differences sorted out as clearly as possible in each subject. Only then can we make guesses about what is likely to interest the children, what it might be important for them to know and — once we have settled that — how we can best teach it. Here, as elsewhere, it is essential to do the thinking first and not rush ahead too quickly with discussing 'methods'. For, as you may see by now, we are not always clear about what our subjects are in the first place or about what it is to teach this or that subject.

6

Education in Controversial Areas

Let us first try to sharpen up a vague chapter title. In certain areas or departments of life, not only do people vary dramatically in respect of their particular beliefs or values, but also there is no general agreement on procedure — on how to handle whole departments — and people are apt to invest in them a good deal of emotion. We shall call these 'ideological' or 'controversial' areas. Examples might include morality, politics and religion. Now, let us try to lay down principles that have to be followed if we are to speak seriously of 'education' in these areas and if we are actually to educate people in them. That sounds like a rather 'abstract' or 'philosophical' approach (as people sometimes say) to a notorious practical problem, but this appearance is misleading. For the main practical obstacles consist, as we see it, precisely in the fact that we either do not want to educate people in these areas or despair of being able to do so. Once we get a clear grasp of what such education would look like in principle, the difficulties of putting it into practice are comparatively small.

It is worth noticing, as preliminary encouragement, that there are several areas that might well be regarded as 'ideological' but (in general) are not, simply because educators have retained sufficient nerve and common sense to keep satisfactory educational practices going. Teachers of science have not, generally speaking (and long may this continue), been so unnerved as to have serious doubts about the educational validity of their subject. One may think that is so because the central features of scientific methodology — what counts as 'doing science well' — are, in fact, tolerably clear.

But it is also true that teachers of English literature, art and other such subjects continue to teach despite the fact that these areas, perhaps more than any others, present great difficulty. Just what does count as being good at literary criticism or musical appreciation? By what criteria do we — if indeed we do — judge some works of art better than others? What principles of reason or standards of success do, in fact, govern aesthetic matters? It is very hard to spell out, or even to be clear about, the answers to such questions, but it is possible to be fairly confident, nevertheless, that in making certain practical moves in education — getting pupils to note the development of character in a novel, or pick out the voices of a Bach fugue, or whatever — we have a kind of tacit knowledge of the area.

We are not saying here that the mere existence of practical consensus guarantees the right educational moves in these areas. We are saying, rather, that our tacit understanding of an area, when suitably clarified, may be quite sufficient to give us a satisfactory start, provided — and with 'ideological' areas it is a big proviso — we are content to stay within the area and treat it for what it is. We get on fairly well with literature and music (generally speaking: we do not deny there are disputes) because we recognize tacitly what sort of business we are in. If somebody starts objecting to the literary merits of P. G. Wodehouse because he broadcast on behalf of the Nazis, or the musical merits of Beethoven because he was a bourgeois, we recognize that he is in a different business, the business of politics. This understanding protects us, though in these ideological days not infallibly, against this kind of category confusion.

We suggest that by 'educating pupils in X', where X is some department of life or form of thought, we should normally be taken to mean at least three things. First, that we show the pupils the appropriate criteria for success in thinking and acting in this department or form of thought, the way in which X comes within the scope of reason — in particular, what counts as relevant evidence for opinions and beliefs. In a word, we encourage them to be reasonable (perceptive, sane, knowledgeable, well-informed, etc.) in X. Not just about X: it is one thing to know a lot (as a historian, or a sociologist, or whatever) *about* mathematics and religion, another thing to have learned to perform well *in* those departments. Second, that we can justify our title 'education in X' (rather than Y) only if we pay particular attention to what is *peculiar* to X as a department or form. Thus 'education in religion' would be at best a misleading title if all we did was to educate children in respect of certain historical or scientific facts (that happened, as it were accidentally, to be connected with certain religions) or in the literary merits of certain religious writings. Third, that we should encourage the pupils to make up their own minds in X, by using the methodology or principles of reason appropriate to it, rather than (or anyway as well as) encouraging them to believe certain conclusions or 'right answers'.

These, it might be argued, follow from what we mean by 'educate', via the connection of that term with what we mean by 'learn'. (The notion of learning marks not just any change but a change in the direction of truth by the application of reason and the use of evidence: see Wilson, 1979b.) In any case, it seems that we are here talking about a coherent and worthwhile enterprise, whether or not it is the only enterprise meriting the title 'education'. Of course, there may be those who do not wish to engage in this enterprise at all, perhaps because they are frightened of the possible outcome, but the chances are that in a pluralistic and shrinking world such people will be driven willy-nilly to pay some attention to it — for instance, to allow some time for 'education in religion', in the above sense, even if they insist on using other time to inculcate certain specific religious beliefs and practices. Our worry is, rather, educators who would like to engage in this enterprise but are unclear about how it can get off the ground.

The main difficulty, we suspect, is that many people only half-believe (at best) that the various titles — 'politics', 'morals', 'religion' and so on — can stand, or be made to stand, for distinguishable enterprises that are *about* something distinguishable and have some sort of distinguishable *point*. We see them rather as arenas in which various combatants do battle, providing material for debate and amusement for commentators but not otherwise engaging in any co-operative or constructive endeavour. That is certainly not an inevitable view: not only Plato and Aristotle but many of their successors as well saw at least some of these fields as enterprises with their own peculiar goods and virtues, somewhat by analogy with the arts and crafts. Less apt to take anything as given, or influenced more by the variety both of particular ideologies and of conceptual systems that the study of history has displayed to us, we feel much more insecure, some philosophers going so far as to claim that the very concepts marked by 'politics', 'morality', etc., are 'contestable', thus putting everything to the service of ideology.

A different approach, however, may make us recover our senses. It is not difficult to see that there is, or might be, a sense of 'politics' such that it is inevitably an important human concern (whatever one's preferences or 'values') and, properly understood, contains within itself a number of non-disputable goods and virtues. Politics, we shall say, is an enterprise concerned with the good of associations or communities (*poleis* in Greek) as such. Not only the need for child-rearing but many other needs (the development of language, for instance, which cannot happen in isolation) make this enterprise inevitable for human beings; and since human beings are always potentially vulnerable to each other, all men must necessarily be concerned with politics — how much is another matter. At the same time, there will be certain necessarily desirable features in a community as such: justice, individual freedom, security and good communications are among these. Anyone who rejected these as goods would have failed to understand what it is to be a human being or what it is to be a member of a community: they are not ideological but logical goods, and the virtues that go with them are also logically required by the nature of the enterprise.

To make this sort of approach conceptually watertight would require much more philosophical argument than is appropriate here. But at least we can see that there are some logical necessities and some concepts that are inherent in politics, around which the pupils' understanding can legitimately be built, and that these have a very different status from those of particular ideologies, current practices or 'values', that happen to be flying around. Thus the ideas marked by 'rules', 'sanctions', 'authority', 'contract' and many others are inalienable, and pupils need to get a firm grasp on them — not only a conceptual grasp, but the kind of grasp best given by practical participation and the assumption of political responsibility (in particular, perhaps, taking the rap for bad decisions or arrangements). If we also give those pupils the attitudes, abilities and skills that are logically required for dealing appropriately with other people in any context — respect for other people's interests, emotional insight, determination and so forth — then they will be equipped to think and act rationally in political contexts, and it will eventually be up to them to decide what practical realizations of the inalienable concepts they think best in this or that situation.

Nor is it difficult to distinguish this approach from one that more or less overtly recommends a particular set of political values. In our own society the most tempting candidate is 'democracy', whatever this may mean; and it is moderately scandalous that most suggested programmes of political education incorporate 'democracy' in a way that takes its value for granted. Still more scandalous, if less naive, are attempts — usually tacit but sometimes overt — to define 'politics' in such a way that other sorts of government (oligarchy, for instance) do not count as political at all. Such moves make it more difficult for pupils and teachers to raise the very important political question of whether 'democracy', in some or all of its senses, is actually a good thing; they are illegitimate from a strictly educational viewpoint, and ultimately impractical because sooner or later pupils will raise the question anyway.

'Health education' affords a similar illustration. Physical health presents comparatively little difficulty, because there is at least a central core of goods that are virtually undeniable — the effective use of one's limbs, freedom from pain and so on. (Though even here moral questions may come in: why not a short life and a merry one? I have not seen the idea of a rational attitude to one's body properly worked out in any health education course.) But mental health requires the same treatment as politics. Either there is an undeniable central core here too, in which case we can at least show our pupils what it is and educate them so that they understand and practise it; or else there is not, in which case there seems little point in imposing our own preferred styles on our pupils — since, according to this view, they are not ultimately grounded in reason.

Again, once we have made the distinction, we can easily list some features of such a core. That a man should recognize objective facts about the world, that he should be free from inner compulsion, that he should be as happy as the world allows him to be — these and other 'values' (and the uselessness of that word emerges in such contexts as this) are such that no reason could be given for denying their general applications. The non-disputable core of 'mental health' is incorporated in the general notion of rationality. To be very sharply contrasted with this are more disputable and specific notions like enjoying one's job (but one might be a slave) or being 'adjusted to society' (but one might live in Nazi Germany). The difference is clear enough; what we have to do is to work out the non-disputable core in more detail and translate it into methods of education.

In these and some other cases we see a way forward. But some areas, or at least their titles, present greater difficulty — a difficulty that relates to the second of the three principles mentioned above. In order to establish a viable and specific area of education, we need to be sure that our titles stand for something tolerably distinctive. We have to be able to distinguish — even though there may be overlaps — between matters of politics and matters of mental health, between politics and morality, between morality and religion. Most educators abandon this struggle and are content to teach very general courses under some extremely vague headings — 'Learning to Live', 'Growing Up' or whatever. Even when the titles in themselves are not as vague as these, the practice itself may be; under 'religious education' all sorts of things may go on that have no distinctive connection with religion.

We may now be tempted to go back on our second principle; for why should this distinctiveness matter? If we can cover all the relevant ground under the broad title of 'Learning to Live', what is the point of these philosophical or classificatory exercises? The trouble is that, without an effective set of categories, we cannot be sure that we are covering all the ground. These 'ideological areas' do exist, though we may be unclear about them; there are important differences, though they do not always appear in the titles. In a similar way we could abolish the distinctions between school subjects or forms of thought and run a succession of classroom periods all entitled 'Life' or 'The Environment', but pretty soon we should have to think about just what the differences were between the various kinds of teaching and learning that we might put under this heading (see chapter 5).

The difficulties with the word 'moral' are notorious, though even here we think it possible to distinguish a number of different enterprises in a strategically sensible way, thus freeing them for educators to put into practice. A better example for our purposes might be the idea of sex education. In so far as this consists merely of biology or other empirical matters, it had better be classified as such. The real question is whether the notion of sexuality gives us a sufficiently distinctive area to justify a distinctive set of educational practices. Thus if one thought that, apart from the biology, anything worth doing under the title of 'sex education' really amounts to the education of emotions that are, in fact, common to the sexual arena and to all or most other arenas of life, then one might prefer to run courses under the title of 'The Emotions' and bring in references to these arenas on the side (sex, friendship, the family, violence and so forth). If, on the other hand, one believed in specifically *sexual* emotions, then 'sex education' would stand for something sufficiently distinctive (see Wilson, 1980).

That may still seem no more than a matter of tactics or title-headings, and certainly it raises the question of what the criteria of distinctiveness are to be. Must we identify a different form or thought, or a different set of goods and virtues? If we can, that might settle it: but there are many successful sets of educational practices that use different criteria — many traditional subjects, for instance, are not distinctive in these ways. Might not a sufficient criterion be that pupils and/or our present society do in fact focus their concern on a certain area, marked by 'sex', or 'war' or whatever? But that would justify *any* concern so focused and would be the natural prey of fashion or ideology (Women's Studies, Black Studies, Disco Studies and so forth). We want something more distinctive and less fragile than that. No doubt some compromise between different sets of criteria will have to be made, if only because some criteria are connected with the pupils' motivation more closely than others. But no compromise will solve our present problems: whatever headings we use, we still have to grapple (as do the pupils) with the question of whether there is something distinctive about 'sexuality' as an educational area and, if so, what it is. We cannot avoid the tasks of getting the concepts clear, whatever we do with the titles.

In much the same way we need to know what may be distinctively put under the title of 'religion': what kind of truth (if any) religious truth is, as against the truths of history, morality and other enterprises. Having determined this, it is then indeed a tactical question how best to organize our time — to decide whether we should have separate periods specifically devoted to this distinctiveness or whether we should allow it and other kinds of distinctiveness to emerge in the study of some general topic or field. But we have to distinguish it in the first place if we are to have anything worth calling 'education in religion' at all. Simply to avoid the charge of indoctrination or to tell the pupils something about religion (or, more commonly, about various particular creeds) is not good enough.

Educators in most liberal societies, at least recently, have been so anxious to avoid the charge of indoctrination that they have (generally speaking) failed even to confront these problems, let alone made a serious effort to solve them. Their continual and (as far as it goes) justifiable concern for 'neutrality', particularly if they are directly susceptible to the political pressures of a pluralist society with many articulate interest groups (pressures that may deter them from even attempting certain 'hot' areas, such as sex or race), has encouraged them to duck the task. In this way they have received much support from a relativistic climate of opinion, which would deny any sense to the idea of a pupil's becoming more reasonable, or perceptive, or well-educated in X, as those terms are normally used. ('Reasonable' for relativists presumably means 'what this or that society takes to be reasonable'. We say 'presumably' because the translation is obviously an inaccurate one, and it is hard to see how any English-speaker with his wits about him could offer it.)

It is very remarkable that, at a time when there is more discussion of the curriculum than perhaps ever before, educators are more than ever unwilling to ask the right questions — questions in the form 'Just what is X?' (where X is the title or potential title of some subject, area, or department). 'How is X different from Y and Z?' 'What is the point of X?' 'What is it to do X well?' It is one thing to compile a general, heterogeneous and impressive list of 'aims and objectives' and to attach them (tenuously) to a title, quite another to make the kinds of distinction we need in order to make sense not only of these 'ideological areas' but of the curriculum generally. Where there is already a satisfactory set of practices attached to a title, and provided (another big proviso) that educators are not swayed to change them by mere fashion, this may not matter too much, but where we have only a set of possible titles, as with the 'ideological areas', the way forward is to try to make the right distinctions.

We are inclined to suspect (though this is no more than a guess) that the causes lie deeper than the desire to cling to one's own values or ideology on the one hand, or despair of any non-relativistic application of reason on the other. These symptoms themselves perhaps indicate a more basic dislike (amounting, when philosophers press the point, to hatred and alarm) of making distinctions and categories in general. It is certainly no accident that our age puts a lot of money on the notion of 'integration', almost as if the mere existence of different categories or the mere fact of separateness and difference were threatening or otherwise intolerable. For consider what we should have to face if and when we got the categories sorted out and properly understood. It would then appear, first, that there were specific standards and criteria that we had to meet in politics, morality, religion and the rest if we wanted to be taken seriously, just as we have to meet standards when doing mathematics or science. Second, it would be evident that some of us were very *bad at* politics, morality, etc., and others of us much more expert — so much more, perhaps, that the idea of entrusting political, moral and other decisions to experts would no longer seem ridiculous. Above all, it would be clear that we could no longer amuse and comfort ourselves by clinging to a set of 'values' or an 'ideology' in a highly general sort of way, because we should be under pressure to assign different 'values' to different categories, where they would fall within the scope of rigorous discipline — just as we cannot now respectably claim to have identified the 'truth' across the board of all the empirical disciplines, for we recognize that 'truth' in mathematics, science, history and other disciplines is different.

There is also, of course, a natural resistance to the whole idea of authority. Thus if one tries to persuade or prove to educators that there is a set of attributes, demanded by pure reason, that anyone seriously concerned with 'morality' (in at least one sense of the term) ought to have and ought to encourage pupils to have (Wilson, 1973), one rapidly comes to appreciate the strength and nature of resistance to any such idea. Very often, if one simply lists these attributes, explains each and shows why each is demanded by reason, such resistance will be very strong. But if one adopts the strategy of asking educators to make their own list of attributes — to write down what, if anything, they honestly believe is required by reason of any serious moral thinker and agent — it nearly always turns out that the lists they make are more or less identical (give or take a bit of terminology) both with the one originally put forward and with each other's. That is hardly surprising, if (as we believe) the items on such a list are glaringly obvious and require no immense intellectual talent to discern. What is more surprising is the intense dislike of being told and any suggestion of 'authority', even if the authority has got it right. That may be a powerful argument for giving teachers and other educators much more autonomy, for putting them on the spot and getting them to face the right questions themselves rather than reacting to the pressures of others.

In the above we have been deliberately brief and have deliberately avoided any direct or sophisticated attack upon those philosophers who, in a way rightly, would challenge us on a good many points. We say 'in a way' because, while it is very important that the classifying and working out of these areas should be carefully inspected and criticized, it is equally important that all those concerned should want to find the best answers they can, and we sense that this desire is often absent. Yet until we have all equipped ourselves with at least a plausible set of views about what a sensible classification would look like and what the criteria of reason or success actually are for each X in each category, it seems largely a waste of time to study the curriculum from the viewpoint of sociology or any other empirical discipline. If we have no clear grasp of what we are trying to do or where we are trying to move towards, we cannot even know what empirical facts are relevant. Does not much — perhaps almost all — of the study of 'curriculum innovation' depend on just what 'innovations' one should be trying to introduce? Social science may not help us much even to identify the opposition unless we know what it is opposition to (see chapter 10). The only way forward, as we have tried to show, is to get clear about the basic concepts and criteria.

7

Accountability

There is always strong (and now increasing) pressure for teachers and educators to be 'accountable'. Is such pressure justified, or is it the result merely of an irrational climate of opinion? And what should 'accountable' mean anyway?

It seems clear that the central issue here, on which most other things will depend, has to do with the *nature of the enterprise*. We need to use some general word like 'enterprise' rather than, say, 'job'; for 'job' may already load the dice by presenting an inaccurate picture of what kind of undertaking we are talking about (rather as talking only about 'skills' in teacher-education suggests that what teachers do and how well they do it is primarily or solely a matter of skill, which is not true). Being a parent is perhaps in some sense a 'job', but not in the same sense that, say, being a bus conductor or a salesman is. We have to agree about what sort of things we are talking about when we talk of (for instance) 'education', 'social work', 'welfare' and so on, for only then can we even begin to get a clear view of the questions (1) who should be empowered to do such-and-such a thing? (2) who has the right and ability to judge whether the thing is being done competently and well? (3) just what counts as doing it competently or well? These lie behind, or represent respectively, the questions: (1) who should be accountable? (2) to whom should they be accountable? (3) just what should they be accountable for? We will return to these questions later.

In categorizing jobs and enterprises we are accustomed to speak of some as involving 'dealing with people' — for instance, being a social worker or a priest or a teacher. Others we regard as concerned more with material products or services, such as being a farmer or a salesman or a sheet-metal worker. That distinction will not do as it stands: doctors deal with people but are very much concerned with material services (medicines and vitamins and so on), and though salesmen have to sell their goods, they have also to deal with people. But behind this idea there lies an important, if rather obscure, dimension, which may be roughly represented by the question, 'How far does this enterprise concern itself with the good of people *as such* or with the good of the "whole person"?' Thus at one end of this dimension we might put enterprises like being a parent or perhaps a housemaster in place of a parent at a boarding school: in these cases the enterprises involve a very general, non-specialized concern for the welfare of children. At the other end, someone may be concerned with mending the school furniture or making sweets that the children will buy; though these jobs contribute in specific ways to the children's welfare, they are not concerned in any overall way with the children as such.

The criterion here is not, surely, just a matter of how general or specific the service is. For we regard some parts or aspects of people as more *central* to them than others. A parent is not just someone who combines the roles of furniture-mender and sweet-maker and cook and nursemaid and so forth but is also — indeed, primarily — someone who is concerned with the child as a being in his own right, as an end in himself; someone who loves him, talks to him, understands his point of view and cares for him as for another human being. A parent does not just dispense services. He may farm the child out, as it were, to others who will in fact dispense particular services better than he can — to a doctor if he is ill, to a teacher if he needs to know something that the parent cannot teach him — but he retains an overall concern.

The centrality of some aspects of a person — his point of view, general attitude to life, psychological state and need for some kind of unconditional love or at least acceptance — makes it difficult to regard some jobs as specializations that can neglect these aspects. Someone who sells me a sweet or a cup of tea need not take me seriously as a person (though often, even in such cases, there may be an important kind of personal interaction: if tea ladies in hospitals were replaced by machines, a lot would be lost). But there would be something wrong in trying to argue, for instance, that because a village priest is concerned only with the souls of his parishioners, he is therefore a specialist and unconcerned with people as such, for there is a clear overlap, at least, between whatever we mean by 'souls' and 'people as such'. Similarly, in practice, and we think necessarily also in theory, it is hard to see how the enterprises of promoting health (manned by doctors) and law-abidingness (policemen) could flourish if the promoters were unwilling, in some degree, to treat people as such rather than just as 'cases'. For being healthy and law-abiding are too closely connected with the central aspects of being a person to make such severance plausible.

If we consider the enterprises marked by such terms as 'education', 'social services', 'welfare', 'youth work' and others, we are bound to admit that they come fairly near that end of the dimension: in other words, the nature of the enterprise in each case involves a concern with the 'whole person' or 'people as such' rather than the dispensing of specialized services. Of course, different enterprises, even of this kind, have some specificity (education, for instance, is specifically concerned with people as learners); nevertheless, they have to take the 'whole person' into account. One can train, or instruct, or 'socialize' people with an eye solely on some particular aim — that they may become competent nurses, or know how to operate a machine, or keep the rules of a particular society — but one can (logically) *educate* them only if one adopts a much more general policy towards them (Wilson, 1979b). Similarly, a person's 'welfare', if we take the term seriously at all, may include being fed and clothed, but it consists of a good deal more than that.

Because of this generality, such enterprises cannot be computerized, or packaged, or even — in a narrow sense of the term — 'administered'. What parents do for their children or lovers do for each other can, of course, be facilitated and encouraged and supported. Mortgages can be made easy, out-of-the-way park benches constructed by benevolent town councils, baby-minders provided, contraceptive information distributed and so on. The point is not that parents and lovers do not need to plan and organize — general enterprises cannot be conducted by spontaneous and unpredictable initiatives alone — but that there is a very severe restriction on the degree to which anyone else can plan, organize or 'administer' *for* them. They have to do it for themselves — of course, with whatever help they can get, but still for and essentially by themselves. The most we can do for parents and lovers in any restrictive (as against facilitating) way is to ensure that they do not cross certain lines, that they do not batter babies or commit rape. Just because the goods are not packageable, we have to avoid laying down guide lines that are too specific, otherwise the relationship becomes corrupted: parents are forced to behave in accordance with the Party handbook or lovers in accordance with a set of conventions forced on them by the pressure of elders or their own peers.

If we want such general enterprises to go on, then, it seems that we have necessarily to *trust* those who undertake them with a good deal more scope, and therefore a good deal more power, than we give to those undertaking more specific enterprises — necessarily, because the nature and structure of general enterprises require it. This puts a good deal of psychological pressure on us, particularly in certain historical periods or climates of opinion. Trusting people with power, in these important areas, is certainly a very unfashionable idea in liberal societies today; indeed, the upsurge of interest in 'accountability' may itself be a symptom of our alarm or reluctance. We compensate for our lack of trust in various ways: by electing supervisory committees or enlarged and more active boards of governors, by imposing bureaucratic and administrative restrictions or even by applying the pressure of pseudo-democratic evaluation (for instance, student evaluation of professorial performance in universities). All these are essentially methods of *not* getting as competent a person as we can and letting him get on with his job.

Naturally, this has consequences of various kinds, not much less disastrous than the corruption of science by the Party line or the corruption of free religious debate by the threat of inquisition. For 'democratic' pressures — the pressures of increased 'participation', a 'general consensus', more and enlarged committees, a more complex bureaucracy and a politicized situation in which the most energetic and persuasive tend to get their way — can be just as crippling as orders from a dictator. It becomes apparent that we have lost faith in the enterprise by failing to trust those who man it and failing to decentralise or delegate the power. People who are genuinely anxious to undertake the enterprise become overloaded and disheartened and move elsewhere, or else reluctantly accept job descriptions that are inadequate for the enterprise (for instance, 'surviving as a teacher in a centralized and bureaucratized state school system' rather than — to put it briefly — 'being entrusted with the power to educate'). First-rate people, understandably impatient of such restrictions and distrust, turn to other fields where they can preserve more independence: their second-rate substitutes accept centralization more deferentially.

Along with the failure to trust goes a fashion for 'integration'. We feel lonely, perhaps, and envious as well as suspicious if small, decentralized enclaves are encouraged or even tolerated: they must be 'comprehensivized', 'integrated', 'rationalized'. Having done this, we then face the other way and become (justifiably) nostalgic about the small village school, the cottage hospital, the family doctor and the local policeman on the beat, alarmed about oversized schools and universities, high-density housing, 'rationalized and co-ordinated' welfare services. Egalitarianism, as well as the (supposed) economic gain of the large-scale, plays a part here; so too does an increasing feeling of impotence on the part of the small and the unattached in a world increasingly dominated by the large. The small trader, the man with no union or only a small one, the semi-independent school or college, the decentralized and apparently anomalous welfare organization — all these, when the economy is rocky and political bullying common, rightly feel insecure and seek protection in larger, more socially orthodox groups with enough muscle to survive.

(1) If this general picture is acceptable, one fairly obvious point follows: these enterprises can be wielded effectively only by those who know the people whom the enterprises serve. What a person's interests consist of, in cases in which those interests are not specifiable and uniform as between one person and another (as clean air or fluoridated water are), can be determined only by someone who knows that person in a fairly intimate way. In education, for instance, there would be something ridiculous about trying to determine a suitable curriculum, or at least all the elements of such a curriculum, for a student one did not know: what is in general valuable for society or for the individual may be tolerably constant, but there are too many variations in ability, attitude and personality to make detailed prescription feasible. So too in social or welfare work or even in matters of health —

certainly if we include mental health: certain things, as perhaps a minimum living wage and a hygienic household, are uniform, but much else will vary. Even the policeman, if he is wise and not hedged about by too many regulations, will treat different cases differently, for although the law is the law, crime prevention at least demands great flexibility of approach.

This means, as in a way we know already but in practice forget, that power must lie with those on the spot, not — except within very broad limits to prevent gross abuse — with supervisory committees or other higher authorities. Sometimes this still happens: it is essential that the surgeon actually in charge of a case, or actually performing the operation, is served by (and is not the servant of) hospital committees, or porters, or administrators, or bureaucrats, or the Patients' Protection Society or anyone else. But usually bureaucracy dominates: teachers are not in control of education, since they cannot plan their own schools, organize their own curricula, exercise whatever disciplinary sanctions they think fit and act with parental or near-parental powers — all of which, quite clearly, are necessary for anything properly called education. They are hired by the local authority or school board; they are deferential to parents and at the mercy of politicians: whereas any adequate conduct of the enterprise of education would involve, rather, their being given service by these parties and (in some conflict) exercising power over them (Wilson, 1977).

Those who know and deal with the clients must, then, be those who are accountable. This accountability must obviously go with the power necessary to do the job: otherwise they will be not so much accountable as vulnerable, as teachers in fact now feel themselves to be and, indeed, largely are. Not many teachers feel accountable or responsible for ensuring that their pupils do not bully, vandalize or in general cause trouble outside the school — and who can blame them, since their hands are tied, and they are more likely to feel worried about whether some pupil's parent will abuse them, if not actually sue them at law? How can the New York police feel accountable for the crime in that city, when legal and judicial regulations make it impossible for them to do more than fight a running, and apparently a losing, battle? How can social workers feel accountable for their ability to cope with their charges, when they are allowed only to offer vague kinds of 'help' in a tender-minded way and forbidden to make their clients do anything at all? Compare all these cases with the admittedly extreme but sufficiently analogous case of being a parent, and we can see what is missing.

(2) To whom should teachers be accountable? Part of the answer to this must, we think, be 'to nobody' or 'to nobody but themselves (and their consciences)'. For since they alone know their clients, and since some of the benefits they aim to produce are intangible and in practice largely unverifiable, what else can we do but hope to select and train people who will do their best? To whom (again) could parents be accountable? Is it suggested that psychiatrists, or priests, or husbands be made to render account to the Minister for Mental Health, or the Department for Religious Affairs, or the Marriage Guidance Council? This would immediately deperson-alize, and hence corrupt, attempts to be a good psychiatrist or priest or husband.

But this point has to be modified in at least two ways. First, there are limits to the freedom of such people. There are some things that we can say, although with caution (and, one might hope, as a result of proper reflection rather than in response to fashionable climates of opinion), some things that they must do, and some that they must not, in any circumstances (teachers must not torture children; priests must take their church services; social workers must not blackmail their clients; and so on). Some degree of accountability is in place here. Secondly, some of the benefits that they dispense are for the good of society, not (or not only) for the good of the individual (whom they alone know), so that society is justly entitled to ensure that its demands — if the demands are just — be satisfied. Thus it is reasonable for any society to insist that whatever else teachers do, they must do their best to ensure literacy, employability and a reasonable degree of conformity with social norms, since without these, as without the willingness to defend the state and some other aspects of social contract, society cannot survive at all.

Accountability in both cases is, quite properly, to society — that is, eventually, to the sovereign power in the state (which, we hope, represents the general will). Effective intermediaries, however, are professional bodies (for instance, the British Medical Association), to whom such accountability is often better acknowledged. For such bodies contain, or should contain, people in the same business, who have themselves done practical work in classrooms (hospitals, etc.) and are aware of the nature of the enterprise; if they do not indulge in sheer sadism or out-and-out negligence, people who do not have this experience will find most cases difficult to adjudicate.

There is something to add here, perhaps not strictly about 'accountability' but about the limits of such enterprises. In many cases we might be inclined to say that the enterprise, or part of it, should be conducted on a voluntary basis, that education, or psychotherapy, or 'welfare', or pastoral care should not be forced on people. We may, perhaps, legitimately force them to conform to a minimum of social norms, in order to get them to pull their weight and not upset other people: and, more doubtfully, we may legitimately force minors or lunatics in their own interest. But that by no means covers all the ground. In these cases, it seems that we should adopt the principles of the open market: that is, those who engage in the enterprises should be able to do so only in so far as the clients (patients, students, etc.) actually ask them to do so — only in so far as there is a demand. They would be, in that sense, 'accountable' to their clientèle: not in the sense that they would be forced, by some higher authority, to submit to their clientèle's evaluation — an absurdity, since *ex hypothesi* the clientele does not know much (or, indeed, anything) about the enterprise and hence cannot judge its practice — but simply in that if they do not attract and retain a demand, they will have no job to do.

In the case of education this is, perhaps, reasonably clear. There are (a) rules, which are binding on all teachers, designed to prevent gross abuse (e.g. sexual assaults on their pupils); there are (b) demands legitimately made by society (e.g. a minimal literacy and understanding of the law); and there is (c) the rest (probably most) of the whole enterprise of education. Teachers must be accountable in respect of (a) and (b), the rules and demands and, for those areas (only), can be seen as public servants in some straightforward sense, perhaps requiring inspectors or overseers to ensure that they keep up to the mark. For the third (c) teachers can be accountable only to themselves (and, in the narrow sense described above, to their own clients, if we think that some or all of this area should be conducted on a voluntary basis). In the case of other enterprises almost everything, again, turns on the nature of the enterprise (see below).

(3) For what should they be accountable? As we said earlier,

unless we get clear about what is to count as 'youth work', 'welfare' and so on, there is little hope of answering this question (or the other two questions), and that is a task not fully to be undertaken here. But we can perhaps see how some of the distinctions made above might help us. Thus if I were a social worker, I should need to know (a) just what abuse-preventing rules I was working within (am I allowed to hit/seduce/swear at/give drugs to my clients or not?) and (b) just what social demands I had to meet (am I to ensure that my clients work, do not sleep rough, do not spend too much time in public libraries, etc.?). Once I was clear about these points, for which I would be accountable to my employers or some higher authority, I should then hope to be able to deal with my clients in all other respects *as I myself thought best* (since I would know them best), though of course with advice and help from outside. But I could not do this with any feeling of security if I were not first clear about the limits of accountability.

Asking for such clarity is, of course, dangerous, since those who make rules and regulations designed to prevent abuse or to ensure the legitimacy of social demands are apt to overdo it; the result is far too many rules, which make it impossible for those who conduct enterprises to do the job effectively (the police are a fair example). A great deal depends here, as we have been insisting throughout, on the willingness of society in general to decentralize sufficiently to realize that we have to trust people with power. Naturally, this is risky: it is, in a way, easier to pass a general rule about, say, the illegality of corporal punishment for children than to accept (as any sensible parent knows well enough) that sometimes some pupils need the odd slap or shaking and to trust teachers not to overdo it. Similarly, fears of sexual abuse have led some educational bodies to promote the rule: 'Do not touch or handle the children physically' — plainly an absurd rule, since in many cases children positively require this. We need clarity in setting the limits of accountability, but the clarity must stem from a proper appreciation of the enterprises.

Those of us who are not obsessed with fears about power, 'paternalism' and 'authoritarianism' are likely to believe that a proper understanding of these enterprises, taken together, will lead to the realization that a great many people are not, in fact, capable of surviving autonomously and happily in a complex modern society. They need looking after, not only (not even primarily) by a set of specialized services — 'education', 'police', 'welfare', 'social work' and so on — but rather, at least in the first place, by one or two people who are responsible for them in an overall way, somewhat in the manner of a parent or village priest or a housemaster. The multiplicity of social services dazes most people at the receiving end; nor is communication good enough for them even to know, let alone understand, just what these services are. They need, above all, some one person whom they *know* and *trust,* someone who always has time for them, to whom they can talk freely and on whom they can rely. If this is paternalism, then paternalism is what we need.

Naturally, such a person could not operate without some abuse-preventing rules and social demands; but it is clear that, to do such a job at all, his powers would have to be pretty wide. He would not be able to operate in any very 'democratic' way or spend much time on committees, and he could not be hampered by bureaucratic procedures. In such circumstances there is some hope that he could begin the task of forming what many people (perhaps all of us) clearly need, something like a genuine community to replace the shapeless, sprawling and dazing world in which we compel, in effect, even the cretinous, the terrified, the senile, the psychopathic and the otherwise incompetent to live, a community that could offer protection and a higher degree of fraternity than mass society (whatever its ideology) seems able to provide. The price of such a community, of entrusting more power to those who run these enterprises, is not the loss of liberty, for the suggestion is not, of course, that such people should seize such power by a *coup d'état* but that the rest of us should have the sense to entrust them with it, of our own free will. The price is that we must recover our nerve and cease to insist on centralization, bureaucracy, excessive restrictions, undue 'participation' and the whole alarmist apparatus that we now seem to have. Mechanisms can exist for unseating those to whom we entrust power or for enabling us to choose those under whose protection we want to shelter, but that is a different matter from constant 'democratic' pressure.

If we take such phrases as 'social welfare', 'community work', 'educating people' and 'pastoral care' seriously at all — and sometimes one feels that these are just a kind of conscience money paid by liberals who cannot control even the most obvious defects in their society — then someone has to be in a position to put a stop to such defects: to prevent bullying and vandalism in schools and out of them, to make towns safe for anyone to walk about in at night, to ensure that old-age pensioners are not terrorized or totally isolated, to enforce obedience to the authorities and to take immediate measures against poverty, homelessness and disease. Even to put this in general terms ('poverty', etc.) is dangerous: it implies that 'society', or some nebulous 'we', can improve matters only through some long-term and large-scale programme of social research and development, whereas what is needed is a person or people empowered to produce immediate and direct deterrents and benefits when needed — again, more or less as a competent parent or housemaster can. Anything short of this results in talk, reports, delay, 'concern', consultation and other symptoms of a society that has lost its nerve; and despite all these, things just get worse.

The truth is that for these obvious and major ills *nobody* is at present accountable. We do not say, 'On such-and-such a housing estate there is a good deal that is wrong. Children are left alone; there is no discipline in the schools; vandalism is rife, violence common. We will appoint a few people with wide powers to clean this estate up, give them whatever money we can afford and let them get on with it, subject only to some abuse-preventing restrictions.' We are frightened that the authority of such people will not be accepted or that they will abuse it. But for such cases (and they are many) such authority is absolutely required: to refuse it is to reject any serious attempt to solve the problems. So we offload the problems on 'society', the current repository of all problems, and think that by 'social change' we can somehow avoid the direct confrontations and negotiations that the enterprises demand: rather as a lunatic parent might think that as long as he provides a 'good social background' for his children, he does not need parental authority to punish, sympathize, help, share, insist, cuddle and do all the things that only a person in some fairly intimate relationship can do.

We are not hopeful that these (very rapidly sketched) points will be agreed; or, if agreed, acted upon in the near future. The fear and resentment of authority lies very deep in early childhood and can easily be fostered (as it has been) in an egalitarian climate. It is more likely that if things get much worse, sheer necessity will force people to accept certain authorities: they may come to accept the protection of any group or institution that can offer it, rather as at the breakdown of the Roman Empire people turned to the large landowners who could at least provide food and military defence. Once certain long-established authorities, norms and contracts are resented or abandoned, it is difficult to re-establish them. Perhaps, as already happens to some extent (notably in the USA), those with enough money to do so will create their own enclaves, with their own guards and security systems, their own power-sources and no doubt, in due course, their own doctors and serfs, while the poor are abandoned to the chaos of an ungoverned society. Or, to use another example, the rich and determined may send their children to independent schools where order is maintained, while the poor and socially incompetent will be able only to abandon theirs to giant institutions deserving the title bear-gardens rather than schools.

Unfortunately, the political system of liberal societies is not such as to make it likely that governments will act definitively in such matters. We know, for instance, that a strong-minded government (and we might expect to find such a one behind the Iron Curtain) would do something that would effectively prevent football hooliganism, ensure a reasonable degree of discipline in schools and keep public order, but we make an unnecessary connection between this (wholly proper) tough-minded use of authority and the (often absurd) ideology and narrow-minded tyranny that are associated with it. It is as if men can retain their nerve only by swallowing some overall and absolute authority with divine or charismatic elements. But we can, of course, in complete freedom and by using no more than reason and common sense, state clearly what we want and do not want in our society and can adopt such authoritative methods as may be necessary to achieve it. We simply do not raise these points or do not communicate with each other sufficiently well to reach practical agreement, and that can only be because we suffer from the kind of fantasies already described. But it is to be hoped that teachers will both see clearly that they need much more power and autonomy in order to do their jobs properly and — either through their unions or by other methods — fight hard until they get such power and autonomy. For without them, serious education is barely possible.

8

Selection

If we are going to have schools or other educational institutions we inevitably face problems about how pupils are to be allocated to them and how they are to be allocated to different groups within them. These problems are often discussed under headings like 'integration', 'segregation', 'comprehensive education', 'mixed-ability teaching', 'setting', 'streaming', 'banding' and so on, but they are best described as problems of selection. Can anything both general and helpful be said about what criteria we should use?

We think it can, but we want first to remind the reader of those particular benefits or goods in which we are interested as educators: namely, benefits directly derived from learning (see chapter 2). The criteria of selection that are appropriate to these benefits are not necessarily the same as those appropriate to other benefits. To take an example from another sphere: if we were selecting a team of chess-players for a top-grade international competition, we should naturally want to select the best chess-players. But it might be that some other nation would be mortally offended if the team did not include some members who were coloured, or Catholic, or women. Thus there would, or might, be a conflict between criteria of selection derived simply from good chess playing and criteria derived from the importance of politics, or diplomacy, or whatever we would want to call it. How we settle such conflicts would depend on the comparative importance of the goods in either category. But we need to be clear — as, in this case, it would be extremely clear — both about the difference between the two sorts of goods and about the criteria of selection appropriate to each.

We shall have to restrict our concern to educational goods and the educational activities that promote them. Here there are some strictly logical points to be made. For any activity A, we may formally say, there will be constituent criteria C such that, without C, A is logically impossible. Since activities necessarily involve people doing things, all people engaging in A will need the ability and willingness to satisfy these criteria (call this 'personal ability/attainment and motivation', PAM). Therefore all As require PAM, via C. For instance, let A be 'playing football': then C will consist of the minimal criteria for the playing of football (the keeping of certain rules, in particular), and PAM will consist, for instance, of knowledge of these rules, the desire to abide by them most of the time, the physical ability to move about and so on.

This is worth stating formally, if only to drive home the point that we are not here talking about 'keeping up standards' or doing things well, the desire for which may be one inspiration of educational ideologies sometimes labelled 'traditionalist' or 'élitist'. We are concerned not with these or any other ideologies but with something much more fundamental: we are talking about what is logically required for things to be done at all. Thus a group of pupils who could not or would not play musical instruments pretty well, follow scores, etc., could not do anything seriously to be described as 'playing Beethoven'; pupils who did not know much Latin and Greek could not be described as 'appreciating classical literature'; and so on. It is not that their skills could only be described as mediocre; rather, it would make no sense to give these descriptions to what they were doing — just as we should not call it 'playing chess' if someone quite ignorant of the moves and pieces pushed chessmen around the board.

These simple points are worth remembering because it seems abundantly clear that whom we select ('segregate' or 'integrate'), when and for what purpose will depend entirely on what activities we want to go on. If we want As that require PAMs that are possible for only a very few (Olympic pole-vaulting, for instance), then no argument is needed: the PAMs will be very hard to achieve, but they are logically required for the As. Similarly, if the A is less demanding, as perhaps in 'learning to read', 'learning about numbers', 'learning about the environment' and so on (compare 'reading Sophocles', 'doing differential calculus' and 'taken pollen counts'), the nature of the PAM follows from the definition of the A. So it seems that the most sensible way to go about this business is first to determine what As we want to go on in education and then see what PAMs these require; and this exercise in itself should settle many issues about selection by reference to straightforward logic. Once we have decided that we want a particular educational activity, A, to go on, the learning groups select themselves: anyone with the relevant PAM can (and, if we think the A to be universally valuable, should) engage in the relevant A; conversely, no one without it *can* engage in that A. Criteria of other kinds (social class, wealth, colour, parental inclination, etc.) are simply not relevant at all. Thus if we think that an A describable as 'appreciating literature' is educationally valuable for all, and the PAM for this is 'being able to read to standard S', then anyone with this PAM can and should do A, and no one else can. It may be said that, for instance, the irrelevant criterion of wealth (perhaps being rich enough to live in a 'desirable' neighbourhood with a 'good' school) does, in fact, segregate pupils in a way that prevents the operation of the proper criterion: that is, pupils who do in fact have the relevant PAMs are not able to engage in the relevant As. But this is simply to point out that we are using the wrong criteria, no doubt because of some kind of social injustice that hinders 'equality of opportunity' — that is, the giving of all pupils *with appropriate PAMs* the chance to do A.

It is not accidental that in educational practice we recognize the obvious force of the logic above most easily in areas that have a clear and definite structure. In many schools it is the mathematicians above all who are in favour of 'setting', 'streaming', etc., partly at least because it is quite clear that mathematics involves stages of learning and that pupils must have gone through one stage successfully before they even begin to tackle another (we have to learn to add before we can multiply and so forth). But all subjects have some conceptual structure of this kind (think of the concepts with which a pupil must be familiar and the understanding he has to possess in order to make sense of an Act of Parliament, Newton's Laws, the trade winds, a sonnet), and there is an enormous job to be done, in each subject, by way of mapping out these structures. Mathematics is not a unique case. This is the danger (whatever may be the advantages) of using very general titles like 'the humanities', 'environmental studies', 'language' and so on. The titles do not, even indirectly, specify just what is supposed to be learned by particular children at particular times. As soon as we get down to specifying this, the particular pieces of learning can easily be seen to be structured and subject to the sort of criteria we are talking about. The danger is that we may never bother to specify in this way.

If we do not even attempt this job, various As that may be important might easily perish by default. For example, suppose an A is described as 'English' in the timetable, such that it has a fairly clear structure, involving fairly specific and perhaps fairly high PAMs at different stages (the ability to learn grammar, correct spelling and punctuation, the desire to understand non-contemporary literature, etc.). Now, suppose we react against this because the PAMs are too high, we think, for the average pupil: we then replace this A by another A (still called 'English') with quite different criteria, more easily satisfied by more pupils (the ability to enjoy some magazine articles, 'creative writing', etc.). In this situation the original A may *simply disappear:* it is not that we are teaching the same thing, 'English', by new methods — we have redefined 'English' to fit what we take to be the average pupil's PAM. The same move may be made with almost any subject title.

Instead of starting with a list of educationally desirable As, trying to get the pupils' PAMs to fit as required and honestly abandoning (for some children anyway) these As where we cannot get the required PAMs, there is a temptation to take some level of PAM (perhaps that of the 'average pupil') as given and then to tailor all our As to fit that level. Thus suppose we have a class of 30 pupils, and we have the option of activities A1, A2 or A3: and suppose that all the pupils can manage A3, whereas only 15 have the requisite PAM for A2, and only 5 for A1. One temptation is to settle for A3, allowing A1 and A2 to go by the board. The opposite temptation involves doggedly persisting with A1, leaving 25 pupils out in the cold. The only way of avoiding both is in some sense to select and overtly to segregate: that is, to arrange for 5 of the pupils to do A1, 10 to do A2 and the remainder to do A3. It is not here relevant whether we do this by putting them in different schools, different 'sets' or 'streams' or different corners of the classroom: the point is that they are segregated simply by virtue of their engaging in a different A.

We want to stress that this leaves certain questions entirely open: in particular, the question of how much value we put on various As. It would be logically possible, if implausible, to maintain that vast numbers of As are not particularly valuable — not only activities that are commonly regarded as 'highbrow' or 'élitist', such as the understanding of Latin and Greek literature, higher mathematics, textual criticism, etc., but also such things as a grasp of scientific method, correct English and computation and an appreciation of good music. These and other examples, if one got down to the business of spelling out the relevant PAMs clearly, would be seen to involve much more specific, and perhaps more demanding, PAMs than we might at first suppose. Those who take their lead from preconceived PAMs might find themselves cutting out more As than they would like. But the move could, of course, be made. Our point here is that the question of whether to make such moves can be settled only by a careful consideration of the As and PAMs we are dealing with — something that rarely happens.

There is one point (we think a strong one) in favour of starting with the As and trying to tailor the PAMs to fit them rather than vice versa — at least as an overall strategy. The point is simply that whereas we can determine the nature (if not the desirability) of As, and hence of the PAMs they entail, just by hard thinking or sheer logic, it is much more difficult to accept PAMs as given or determinate in isolation from any A. First, though it is not, of course, absurd to talk generally about a pupil's 'motivation' or 'interest' in learning, we naturally want to ask 'Motivation for what?' 'Learning what?' As we all know, a pupil's 'motivation' or 'interest' may vary very widely from one subject or activity to another. Secondly, while we cannot do anything practical to alter the logical entailments between various As and PAMs, we can and should do a great deal to alter the PAMs themselves. How much a pupil can 'be motivated' to do or to learn will depend very much on how much 'motivation' we give him.

In this respect we have to guard against not only misleading models of human learning that may be encouraged by the term 'motivation' itself but also certain fashions or prejudices that may unduly limit for us the kinds of incentives or 'motivation' we can in fact bring to bear. One thing that may set such false limits is some kind of theory to the effect that certain motives are bad in themselves, or worse than others, or 'developmentally' inferior in terms of some set of 'stages' leading towards 'autonomy' or 'intrinsic motivation'. It is quite unclear to us that there is any proven, or even any intelligible, theory of this kind; and in any case, one might well be prepared to endure the (hardly intolerable) guilt of using 'inferior' incentives (for instance, fear) in order to produce desirable results (for instance, that pupils should actually learn to read and refrain from bullying or knifing each other). Another quite different point, practical in nature but surely smelling even more of fantasy rather than common sense, is the fact that teachers are simply not empowered to bring certain incentives to bear. This needs to be changed.

In any case, if we did take different pupils' PAMs as given, or to the extent that we did, similar arguments would apply. Because the PAMs are conceptually connected with the As, there will be certain things that any person (with a given PAM) logically cannot do and certain things that he can. Suppose we prefer to start from some idea of 'what suits' the pupils rather than from the idea of certain As being somehow intrinsically valuable: then the As that 'suit' different pupils will necessarily be different simply because of the different PAMs. If one person is not 'suited' by, say, higher mathematics — because his IQ is too low, or because he is bored, or because of whatever we are prepared to take as satisfactory evidence — then another person with a high enough IQ or sufficient enthusiasm or whatever *will* be 'suited' by it. In other words, whether we start with the As or with the PAMs, the conceptual connection between the two drives us to differentiate. People are just, in logic, 'selected' or 'segregated' in this way, whatever practical arrangements one may choose to deal with this, and to turn one's back on this fact altogether implies a refusal to make any educational judgements at all — the claim, in effect, that as we have no idea what As are of any value, or what PAMs pupils have, we might as well lump everything together.

We have seen that any activity demands some selection, but the same point holds good even if we do not wish to engage in *activities* at all. One might imagine a person who dislikes segregation arguing as follows: 'We won't have any "academic" As, like learning mathematics and Latin and so on, because a lot of pupils are not up to this in any serious way. So we'll have very simple As, like swimming and playing games together. Oh, but wait! A substantial minority are mad or crippled. They cannot swim or play games properly. All right, they needn't *do* anything.

They can just *be* together — it's a good thing in itself to have working-class children mixing with middle-class children, blacks with whites and so on. That at least isn't subject to "criteria" that exclude people.' But, of course, it is. We may succeed in mixing working-class with middle-class or black with white, but now, what about redskin children? Have we got enough fat boys in the school? Is there a proper mixture of pretty and ugly girls? Are we not excluding people from the north of England (Irish children, pygmies)? Indeed, is it not exclusive and 'segregationist' to have just children in schools anyway, as we are keeping out adults and keeping in pupils?

Some criteria must apply, because it is logically impossible to use *every* criterion. Even if we say, 'Schools should include everybody', that must mean 'everybody within a certain area'; and even if we go beyond this and import people from abroad, we cannot import them all. Some people, by chance or design, will be left out: and in the extreme case in which nobody is left out, we should not be talking of a particular institution at all — we should be talking of the whole world. Hence we can talk of schools or any other institutions not as 'selective' or 'non-selective' in general but only as 'selective' by reference to some criteria. This (obvious) point is sometimes missed because in many debates 'selection' is given an over-specific meaning. Men are easily bewitched by the specific practices and institutions that are before their eyes; much as 'examination' tends to be interpreted in terms of specific (written or institutionalized) examinations, so that people too readily take up a position for or against 'examinations' without bothering to remember that some form of examination in the wide or non-technical sense would be a necessary feature of any system of sustained or serious learning (for one thing, any serious learner would want to be as clear as possible about how much progress he was making).

Can we even talk of schools as *more* or *less* 'selective' except by reference to specific criteria? It may seem that we can: surely school X, which demands, say, that its entrants should both pass the Eleven-plus and live in the neighbourhood, is more selective than school Y, which simply demands that they live in the neighbourhood. But in practice this distinction is illusory, for we have to assume that the school will fill its places, and then the extent of the 'neighbourhood' will be different. School X will have a wider neighbourhood or catchment area on which to draw, since it will draw only those who pass the Eleven-plus; school Y will have a narrower neighbourhood, since it is committed to taking all the children within it. The addition of one criterion relaxes the force of the other for school X, and the absence of the (academic) criterion in effect makes the criterion of 'neighbourhood' more stringent for school Y.

There is an important point here, worth noting because it does, we think, partly account for the feelings of many people who claim to be 'against selection'. Some rough distinction can be drawn between 'man-made' and 'natural' criteria of selection, and there are many people who resent the former but tolerate the latter. Thus it may seem to such people that the 'man-made' criterion of passing the Eleven-plus is more objectionable than the 'natural' criterion of living in the area. As this example shows, the distinction is often difficult to sustain in practice: there are human or 'man-made' reasons why people live in certain neighbourhoods (e.g. they can get a job or afford a house there) — people do not just grow 'naturally' in neighbourhoods, like wild flowers. It is, in fact, quite hard to think of criteria that are not, or could not be, affected by human action — features which are totally 'natural'. Even such features as height or physical strength or intelligence can at least be diminished or stunted by human behaviour.

But in any case it is not clear why these 'natural' criteria should be preferred. People do indeed differ in, say, their skin colour or their physical attractiveness, and there may not be much we can do about it. But why should these criteria be preferred, in principle, to such 'man-made' criteria as (say) a person's social position or the passing of a certain examination? It may seem that by merely allowing the natural criteria to operate and by not positively enforcing criteria of our own making, we somehow evade the terrifying responsibility (some might think, the guilt) of 'selecting'. But this is clearly an illusion: failure to act, to enforce our own criteria, is as decisive as acting. Thus, to take a parallel, if we allow cattle to become the property of the strongest or the most cunning, rather than enforcing laws of property, this must mean that we prefer the criteria of strength and cunning to whatever other criteria those laws represent. Generally speaking, indeed, we seem to believe that 'man-made' criteria represent some improvement on 'natural' ones.

What other worries could we have about selection in general? For the trend of our argument so far suggests that the only thing we have to worry about, as educators, is the question of what educational activities (As) we want to go on: we can then, as rational beings, select only those people who can profit by these As — that is, those with the relevant PAMs. If we do not, our sincerity in saying that we want those As to go on will be in doubt: just as if someone said that he wanted a Beethoven symphony played well but did not select members of the orchestra by reference to their talent and willingness as musicians, we should question what he originally said. This is, indeed, in broad terms the correct conclusion; but it is important that we should do justice to any doubts that might remain.

The chief worry is represented by an ideal associated with the desirability of 'integration' for the specific educational purpose of what we may call 'moral' or 'social' education. But for this purpose the most natural way in which we should think education relevant, surely, is that educators should have the direct and immediate task of educating their pupils *out of* the domination of irrelevant criteria. We do not, after all, think that a person's identity or self-esteem should turn on his social class, or religious affiliation, or wealth, or whatever social criteria may be current in any particular society. We are talking here about the task of moral education or the education of the emotions, and if we take this seriously at all, presumably the chief message we want to get across is that pupils should not put undue stress on social distinctions, that these distinctions do not ultimately matter, that they should not care too much about whether they are working-class or middle-class, black or white, rich or poor, pretty or ugly. We want them, of course, to acknowledge the facts; if a pupil is bad at mathematics or football, or too fat, or poor, we do not wish to mask these facts or pretend that they are otherwise. On the contrary, it is an essential part of their education that these facts should be faced. Somehow as educators we have both to do this and to give the facts no more than their due weight.

For obvious logical reasons, it is impossible to do this unless (for at least some of the time) we actually attend to these facts and distinctions. For example: in so far as pupils are or may become racially prejudiced, the feelings here have to be brought out into the open and moved in the direction of reason. Little or nothing is educationally gained simply by 'mixing': the pupils have to learn somehow that a proper concept of a person is based not upon race or colour but upon other criteria, that the needs of all persons have to be respected and so on. If they have inclinations that run counter to this rational procedure, these have to be acknowledged and inspected and somehow changed. Of course, it might be possible simply to prevent trouble, 'social divisiveness', race riots or whatever by other means. We could run advertising campaigns with the message 'Black is Beautiful', or paint white people black, or make everyone colour-blind. But that would have nothing to do with education: nobody would have learned anything or developed any kind of knowledge or understanding.

It is, certainly, a significant fact that, for the specific business of moral or social education (as against, say, learning mathematics), the pupils bring their data with them, as it were: that is, pupils in the same school cannot help but learn about each other, the people they actually mix with. But it seems a very open question how relevant this fact is or in what direction it points. If one wished them, for instance, to grasp and apply some notion of 'kindness to animals', what 'mix' of animals would be educationally the most desirable? Would we feel guilt about *only* having hamsters and cats and rabbits, 'segregating' (by accident or design) cows, elephants and aardvarks? Should we feel guilty about *only* having such-and-such a range of pupils, within which there will certainly be plenty of variation in terms of age, personality, appearance, taste and so on, and not 'integrating' morons, pygmies, aristocrats and (if we can find any) Martians? If so, our guilt is logically endless.

This does not mean that it makes no difference what 'mix' we have. For example, we might wonder whether the pupils would really grasp the concept of 'kindness to animals' if they only had one kind of animal — say, hamsters: might they not grasp only 'kindness to hamsters'? So too, if they only had one kind of fellow-pupil; for lack of experience and interaction, they might not find it easy to grasp the concept of a person if the only people they ever saw were (say) clean-faced Catholic girls of an obedient disposition. But all this is uncertain and turns very much on what we ought (for this purpose) to count as 'one kind of'. It is too easy merely to assume that the criteria of differentiation *we* are worried about (colour, creed, class) are the ones that form the chief impediments to pupils' moral development, and that we best overcome these impediments by having a 'mix' that does not use these criteria. A lot of empirical research needs to be done, but we are inclined to think that educational success here turns on quite other factors, mostly to do with methods of moral education that are more general in character.

A second worry is that the application of certain criteria of selection makes substantial numbers of pupils feel like 'failures', destroys their self-confidence or prevents it from developing, type-casts them as failures, an image that they then live up to, gives them misguidedly low expectations, etc. Since learning any activity, as we have seen, necessarily involves some acknowledgement (however disguised) that certain people have higher attainments than others — some know X already, others have not reached the stage at which they can even start learning it and so on — the argument must presumably point to some much more general sense of failure, perhaps springing from, or (more likely) symbolized by, 'academic' failure in schools, but going far beyond that. Merely the realistic recognition of one's own abilities and attainments, whether in learning or in other things, cannot be wrong; and if this (obviously desirable and anyway inevitable) recognition develops into a general sense of failure, the clear implication is that schools are failing to educate their pupils in other ways.

We must, again, remember that since some kind of selection (by the application of some criteria) is logically inevitable, the argument must presumably be taken to refer to the specific criteria currently under fire: e.g. in the UK different types of secondary school, 'setting', 'streaming' and so on — that is, selection by ability, or attainments, or (correlating with these) social class. The argument must therefore make the assumption that a pupil's or adult's 'self-image', 'self-confidence' or 'sense of being valued' is primarily dictated by his social position. The line is that whether I 'feel a failure', 'value myself', etc., will turn first and foremost, on such things as whether I pass the Eleven-plus examination, or am in the 'A' stream, or am a member of a particular social class, or make a lot of money. Some of these (the last, perhaps) are more plausible than others; none, to my mind, is very plausible, and certainly none is proven. Sociologists will, of course, stress social factors; that is their trade, and such factors are easier to point to. But we are here talking about psychological states of mind, and psychologists would point, much more plausibly, to such causal factors as loving parents, good pupil—teacher relations, adequate personal relationships and so forth. One might reasonably suppose that the amount of 'self-confidence' or 'sense of failure' in people is reasonably constant or at least depends on basic psychological factors, and that particular social systems and distinctions simply give it a certain form — in the UK I worry about not being upper-class, in the USA about not making enough money, in ancient Sparta about not being brave or strong enough, in monasteries about not being holy enough, and so forth.

We do not, of course, deny that in some sense a person's valuation of himself is 'dictated by his social position'. If the term 'social' is stretched far enough, to include (for instance) his infantile relationship with his mother, or the question of whether there is a kind teacher to take an interest in him, then it would make no sense to deny it: 'social' is now being used to cover any source of influence except the genetic. But in a more normal sense, which relates roughly to the general structure of the larger society rather than to the smaller groups of which the person is more immediately a member, the proposition is at least highly dubious. Do we, in fact, believe that any reasonably sophisticated notion of 'valuing oneself' could be due to 'social' factors in this sense? It is not, after all, until many formative years have passed that the child is seriously aware of such factors.

It should strike one here that our uncertainty about this is, once more, due to our regarding the problem as a social rather than an educational one. If we were really concerned with 'a sense of failure', 'self-confidence' and so on, we should have a clearer idea about how these could be generated and, in consequence, a clearer idea about the sorts of groupings (in schools, houses or tutor groups, or elsewhere) that would be suitable. Thus one might advance the idea of grouping pupils according to psychological type, on the analogy of mental hospitals: we might have one group for the over-confident or bumptious or arrogant, another for the depressed and the downcast. Or perhaps, thinking now of successful achievement, we should want to keep those of similar PAMs together, since those of very low PAM would find it hard to succeed at anything in the face of competition from the more able and competent. It might, indeed, turn out that how they were grouped made little or no difference, but rather that everything depended on certain kinds of personal relationships and attitudes on the part of the staff.

These first two worries have close connections with a third, couched in terms of prejudice, inter-group hostility or 'divisiveness'. One of the more curious assumptions here seems to be that the more you 'integrate' or 'mix' people, the more distinctions are abolished, and this too seems psychologically naive. There are two possible weaknesses here. First, the distinctions may simply change: for instance, we mix social classes only to find that 'socially divisive' groups arise based on different criteria (as, for instance, style of dress or taste in music), and these groups may be hierarchical, so that general self-confidence is not improved. Second, the initial distinctions may simply be reinforced: if (say) a tenderly nurtured set of upper-class pupils mixes with a more toughly nurtured set of working-class pupils, it is not at all clear that the result will be to produce mutual understanding and admiration — the effect may simply be to reinforce or even to generate prejudices and stereotypes, to drive each group in on itself and to produce greater defensiveness and even paranoia. (It is not obviously true, to use other examples, that the more men mix with women, the more they like them; that the more international sport is played, the more international understanding is advanced; or that the more time big boys spend with little ones, the more they learn to admire and respect each other.) Clearly, much — we think almost everything — will depend on the way or context in which the 'integration' or 'mixing' is done. Perhaps it would be more efficient simply to accept the groups that pupils *themselves* make (which would certainly involve criteria such as common interests and lifestyle, no doubt connected with social class) and work on those: we might get further by accepting differences between groups and classes and making special educational arrangements to ensure that pupils of one group mixed with those of another whenever we thought educationally desirable — perhaps not very often, but often enough (if, indeed, frequency of contact is relevant) to ensure that they recognized and respected each other for what they were.

Naturally, this is a matter of empirical research, but no competent research is likely to be conducted unless we agree about what counts as success. We have somehow to get away from the fantasy that the mere existence of different groups, 'selection', 'barriers' and so on is somehow bad or disreputable. There is, we suspect, a feeling that even if we all succeeded in educating our pupils to feel self-confident and to respect the worth of other human beings, we should somehow have failed if they then chose, as adults, to live in separate social groups, pursuing their own interests and not mixing much with those whose interests were different. Behind this is not only the idea that 'Walls divide and must come down' (compare 'Good fences make good neighbours') but also a deep feeling of isolation and insecurity; as if, by breaking down barriers and sweeping everything together, we could somehow achieve more conviviality, or fraternity, or love. But love, like every other human enterprise, depends as much on the maintenance of rules, criteria and some degree of segregation as upon 'breaking down barriers'. We have just to pick the right criteria.

Part of the trouble here, surely, is an obsession with social class, evident in the identification of pupils by criteria quite irrelevant to *educational* aims (for instance, as 'working-class' or 'middle-class'). Even intelligent sociologists get into all sorts of contortions in their endeavours to avoid saying what is plainly true, that in certain (perhaps educationally important) respects most working-class pupils are inferior to most middle- or upper-class ones — for instance, as regards their use of language. Right-wing authors who proclaim the right of middle-class parents to have their children brought up in middle-class values are, of course, no better. Both are infected with the idea that education involves some kind of social battle. As we know quite well, there are certain skills and competences in language-using that are educationally important, and there are certain procedures in morality or practical action that need to be taught to children because they are reasonable procedures. How far the use of these competences and procedures correlates with social class (or height, or hair colour) has no relevance whatsoever to educational aims; nor, we think, much relevance to educational practice. Any competent subject-teacher will want to know, not the socio-economic rating of his pupil's parents, but how far he is advanced in that subject and how he can be made to advance further. Part of the trouble, as we hinted earlier, is that certain aims that involve notions like 'sense of failure', 'self-image' and so on do not obviously fit traditional school subjects.

But this difficulty can be overcome by a comparatively slight intellectual effort. The position is somewhat like that of religious education. There are still people who regard such education as essentially a matter of inculcating or passing on some particular faith or creed; whereas, if we can talk seriously about education in religion at all, it should be as absurd to talk of 'Christian religious education' or 'Jewish religious education' as it is to talk of 'Christian mathematics' or 'Jewish physics'. In something like the same way, we have partisans of 'middle-class values' or 'working-class culture'. One is not always sure that the 'standards' defended by right-wingers are standards inherent in the notion of education itself (and hence applicable to all pupils) or the partisan standards of a particular class or creed; equally, it is quite plain that a lot of people are illiterate and stupid and that most of these are to be found in the 'working class'. We can only avoid these idiotic polarities by keeping our eyes firmly fixed on the culture-free criteria of reason. We have to ask and answer the questions: what can we reasonably teach, or what qualities can we reasonably give by educational methods, to *any* child? What is there that is demonstrably *not* tied to the demands of our particular society, creed, class, colour, political beliefs, traditional way of life or personal prejudices? It is particularly regrettable that the same social scientists who complain about certain aspects of 'society' also appear to think (in so far as one can understand this at all) that there can be no answer to these questions because all 'values' are 'culture-bound' or related to particular social norms.

In demanding culture-free criteria of reason, we do not demand that education should pay more attention to the intellect ('academic standards') than to the emotions ('awareness', 'self-confidence', etc.). A serious attempt to lessen the 'sense of failure', to produce more 'achievement motivation', to wean pupils from the use of 'socially divisive' criteria in general (or whatever our aims here may include) would not — we think, logically could not — consist only or even primarily of *sociological* moves. The matter has more to do with more basic notions, among which love is clearly one of the most important. We cannot expect political, social or administrative arrangements to win this battle for us: the most we can hope is that they will facilitate our victories.

9

Staff—Student Conflicts

A cold war, or at least some degree of coolness, is common between staff and students. Occasionally it hots up (via demonstrations, chants, boycotts, occupations, etc.) to maximum temperature, at which point a student may incarcerate himself — or, now that women can join the Marines, herself — in the top of a tower at an American university with a 0.50 rifle and shoot his teachers on the campus. Experience persuades us that the symptoms, causes and cures are common to most or all instances of such conflicts; that the strictly intellectual aspects of the problem yield fairly easily to an elementary knowledge of moral philosophy and psychiatry; and that practice can be improved partly by such knowledge but chiefly by the willingness of both parties to own up to their own emotional states; something easier said than done. We attempt here only the outlines of description and solution.

Symptoms and Causes

We run these two together partly because any distinction between the two is hard to make (a symptom of conflict may itself be the cause of further conflict), but largely because the most important thing is to get the feel — as it were, the psychological tone — of what happens. The first task is to put together a number of points that may help to clarify that tone, and to generate a description that rings true, rather than to attempt any kind of structured causal analysis. Such analysis, is, anyway, likely to be doctrinaire and to result in the various parties adopting fixed positions and attitudes in accordance with the doctrine (the adoption of Marxist roles is an obvious contemporary example) — and this simply entrenches the problem rather than dissolving it.

Rational attitudes are inevitably, or at least characteristically, harder to adopt than personal or autistic attitudes simply because rational attitudes and reason in general involve shelving one's individual passions (sometimes one's individual interests) in favour of some wider and less immediately perceptible good, quelling what Iris Murdoch describes as 'the fat, relentless ego' and trying to emerge from what Plato calls 'the world of sights and sounds'. This point is strengthened when we talk of our reactions to authority: rational or functional authority is something the growing child cannot, in principle, grasp before grasping the much more primitive concepts of authority based on naked power, or charisma of some kind, or uncritical tradition, or an ideology common to both the authorities and clients. Our early understanding and experience of these ultimately irrational or non-rational kinds of authority are, obviously enough, what conditions most of our adult behaviour towards authority in general. When a particular ideology, or set of values, or even just a set of conventions governing the etiquette of social behaviour is no longer shared, it is not surprising that we do not at once remedy the situation by the only possible method — that is, by establishing a new consensus or contractual deal.

We should be even less surprised if we are not clear about the point and scope of particular deals. The kind of rules and discipline required for the effective running of, say, an army, a hospital or a sailing ship are comparatively obvious; and there is, moreover, a fairly immediate and disastrous pay-off if we get the rules wrong — battles are lost, people die on the operating table, the ship sinks. With education this is not so. Some of our confusion is understandable; there is, indeed, room for argument (both conceptual and empirical) about just what the enterprise we mark by 'education' requires — certainly, there are borderline cases and fuzzy areas. But most of it, if understandable (for education has always been a natural arena for the play of fashion, fantasy and metaphysics), is certainly not justifiable. If somebody were to say, for instance, that it does not matter for education whether or not students work as they are told, whether teachers have the power to enforce the discipline necessary for the work to be done, or buildings necessary for that work were occupied, or, conversely, that it does very much matter for education whether or not students wear beards, or are homosexual, or chew gum, then, in default of some sound argument to the contrary (and there may, of course, always be such an argument), one would claim that he has an insecure grasp of the concept of education. He does not understand what education is or is for. He has confused the enterprise with other enterprises of a moral, aesthetic or ideological nature.

Such confusion is, in fact, very common. It is one thing to argue for school uniform, certain styles of dress and language or sexual behaviour on moral or aesthetic grounds, quite another to argue for them on educational grounds. The tendency to introduce our own, or our society's, ideological preferences into education shows how tenuous our desire to educate really is. We are much more concerned to defend or impose our own values. It is not, in fact, very difficult to list those rules that are necessary to, say, the proper running of a university, a college or a school, provided we stick to educational criteria; naturally, as soon as politics, or morality, or any sort of personal ideal is allowed a free hand, there is no limit to conflict and no secure area of co-operation. The position is like one in which two individuals or corporations refuse to trade with, say good morning to, or play games with each other because each believes that the other has the wrong religion, skin colour or political beliefs. Of course, nobody (nobody in his senses) would actually prescribe a general principle by which anyone was permitted to interrupt functional enterprises for ideological reasons, but then we do not often achieve the detachment needed to think about the issue in a reasonable manner. We prefer to strike out and make gestures when we can.

When consensus breaks down and there is no contract to replace it, the symptoms are predictable and painful. It is not so much that the various parties are clear-headed about identifying and negotiating their particular interests in a reasonable way; that would pretty rapidly lead to a new deal. It is rather that they strike attitudes and stand on their dignity, the only thing they can cling to if they are to avoid the more extreme feelings of chaos. Gangs labelled 'we' and 'they' are rapidly formed; almost any point, however reasonably advanced, is taken personally; communication becomes increasingly stylized and less informal; and before you know where you are, an issue that could easily be settled in ten minutes over a glass of sherry by a small group of reasonable men fails to be settled by lengthy and arduous meetings of joint committees and by the formal interchange of innumerable pieces of paper. The whole scene becomes at once tragic and laughable: it is above all an unreal scene, a kind of play-acting or mime in which the agents act out their parts in a dream-like way.

Equally classical and reminiscent of early childhood are the symptoms peculiar to each party. The students, perceiving the uncertainty of the authorities, test their limits out (sometimes virtually to the point of destruction), like children gauging how much they can get away with. Whether or not the actual issues have real importance (and, of course, they may), they test for the sake of testing rather than for the sake of the issues — or, rather, for the sake of seeing where they stand and what norms are actually in force. They may do this, again like children, half-playfully or more anxiously and hence more ferociously; even the chants are child-like. The staff, lacking the confidence of ideological commitment and having no alternative rationale on which to rely, at once feel threatened. They have nothing to stand between them and chaos except the orthodox liberal hope that the students want to be reasonable and will become so if they treat them more as equals or make various moves under such headings as 'democracy' and 'participation'. They entertain the fantasy that patience, calm persuasion, clear argument and impersonal adjudication will eventually win the day, though this does not always prevent them from feeling personally attacked and alarmed. In general, they are less clear about whether they should be acting as fathers, elder brothers or equals than the students are about acting as rebellious children, so that the tendency is for the students to gain ground rather than to lose it.

It is important to appreciate that the amount of rational thinking that goes on is much less than either party consciously admits to. What is at stake is a number of highly generalized pictures to which each side is wedded and which become much sharper and painted in much more lurid colours as the conflict continues. Much of what is done and said is symbolic rather than conceived in terms of cause and effect (rather as, in some quarters, independent schools are hated as symbols of 'divisiveness', whether or not they actually cause it). On one side, staff object to long hair, bad language, certain styles of dress and whatever seems to them contrary to a generalized picture of the 'good' student; on the other, there is considerable student resentment of the particular privileges enjoyed by staff that seem to flaunt their authority or status — dining at high tables, having separate common rooms and so forth. Gestures are often symbolic, in that they often have no logical connection with the point of dispute; rather as refusing to attend chapel services is, in some schools, a more or less required form of protest against almost any disliked practice, or being admonished by the headmaster (or even being beaten) a standard ritual for dealing with almost any kind of offender.

But it does not at all follow from this that the phenomena must be seen only in the light of some totally non-rational malaise or social disease, not to be negotiated by reason. That leads to the idea that our best bet is to keep a low profile and by some (any) means to 'avoid trouble' if we are the authorities or that we should keep up some (any) form of pressure if we are the students. Governments characteristically behave like this, paying danegeld to any potential trouble-makers (the praetorian guard, the trades unions with muscle) in order simply to buy them off, without reference to justice or contract. We even prefer to cancel football matches or to prevent some people from attending rather than allow them to attend while ensuring that sufficiently clear and strong rules and sanctions will operate to make them behave properly. There are, of course, devices that authorities can use to inhibit student unrest and devices that students can use (mostly involving collective action) to wear down the staff, but these are irrelevant. They relate to particular fears or desires for particular troubles, not to establishing long-term mechanisms for dealing with potential trouble in general.

Cures

There are two types of cure for these conflicts, both fairly obvious and necessary and to be applied simultaneously. The important thing is to distinguish them.

(a) The more obvious of the two is the establishment of clear, detailed, agreed and enforceable contracts in advance of conflict. Many people dislike the very idea of this, preferring to rely on some general (if nonexistent) consensus about what is 'reasonable' or 'decent'. At one university much that should have been determined by clear rules was, in fact, adjudicated in terms of 'reasonable behaviour'; predictably, what the students regarded as reasonable behaviour was wildly different from what the staff envisaged. Naturally, not everything can be spelled out in terms of rules; but a great deal can, and what is left can be stated to reside within the authority of this or that body or individual. Only then can both sides know what the rules of the game actually are and what is to happen if someone breaks them. Any space left outside the rules is always potentially space for conflict (as, indeed, we see in actual games: it is precisely the absence of rules about behaviour on the tennis court, for instance, that allows the wearisome scenes now so common at tournaments to take place).

Contracts must satisfy four criteria: they must be fair, agreed, clear and enforced. Of these, the most difficult in principle is the first, but in educational matters the difficulty is much diminished. For either (in schools) we regard the clients as minors, which allows the authorities (the educators themselves or other social agencies) to frame the contracts in the light of their own unilateral judgement, though bearing in mind the best interests of the clients, or else (in higher education) the institution is selective — like members of a club, the clients do not have to join and need not sign up if they do not want to. There is no reason against, and many reasons for, allowing different institutions to offer quite a wide variety of different contracts, though of course, since they are all concerned with education, there will be much common ground.

That the contracts should be agreed — and that means, crucially, agreed and signed in advance — is straightforward enough, though it is extremely important that all clients should understand, before signing, exactly what rules they are subscribing to and exactly what sanctions will apply if they break them. That is a matter of making the contracts clear rather than attempting to rely on 'good sense', 'good will' or anything of that kind. There is no harm in spelling out even obvious details: if good will is present anyway, nothing is lost; and if it is not, a great deal of time and energy is saved. Nor is enforcement particularly problematic, particularly since institutions of higher education have the option of simply dismissing any clients who will not play by the rules — an option, we think, that all educational institutions should enjoy (even where education is compulsory), since there is a limit to the possibilities of educating a person against his will.

We give here simply the most obvious elements of the formal framework, since we believe the clarity and firmness of that framework to be more important than the particular content — extreme and improbable cases excepted, of course: just as, apart from cases of gross over-severity or laxness, it is much more important for a growing child that he should have a clear set of parental rules within which he can live than that those rules should be of this or that kind. Naturally, this does not mean that contracts cannot be more or less sensible in content. But there are two general guidelines to help us here. First, there is the criterion or set of criteria offered by the enterprise of education itself, which is what the whole apparatus is for: this we have mentioned already. Secondly, there are principles of natural justice that can steer us away from the purely symbolic or ideological. In fact, these latter are often disregarded: for instance, it seems clearly just that one who causes damage to another should be expected to compensate his victim for whatever damage he has done (that might, indeed, reasonably be taken as the root idea of retribution), so that fixed or token fines appear not to fit such cases. That is perhaps only one rather obvious illustration of the way in which types of sanctions or enforcement have become ritualized or disconnected from the purposes which they serve.

Nor, of course, do we claim that educational institutions are sovereign states: they are given parameters within which to work by other institutions and by society at large. They also have to pay considerable attention to public relations. Just how much attention depends on many variables, one of the most important being the extent to which educators are themselves prepared to be clear about how much power they need in order to educate and willing to fight for it. But this really makes no difference to the formal framework: if certain rules have to be written in for the benefit of public relations rather than on strictly educational grounds, so be it. As long as the rules are clear and their rationale is honestly described, they can legitimately form part of the deal.

All this allows the administration to operate impersonally, without much or any argument; and there are, as we have already hinted, deep psychological reasons why the idea is resisted — apart, that is, from the mere naivety of failing to distinguish this cure from the procedures represented below, which are to do with establishing trust and good communications in general. Liberals as well as anarchists dislike the idea of rules, usually picturing them as restrictive or pedantic rather than enabling (as they also are). Part of the alarm here is the relinquishing of personal wants and judgements to impersonal procedures: rules are seen as 'dehumanizing' (as if the rules of tennis somehow 'dehumanized' the game), even if we build into the rules — as naturally we shall — second-order principles about legitimate methods of changing them. They are felt to inhibit fraternity, as if genuine fraternity itself did not rely on adherence to rules — as if, indeed, it did not partly consist of such adherence. But the main fear, we believe, is fear of separation, particularly on the part of the authorities. In giving orders or enforcing impersonal rules we distance ourselves, if only for a time, from children, students or other clients. We are no longer (we feel) loved or even respected for ourselves, and in the absence of a sustaining and legitimizing authority, we feel isolated and unsupported. Liberals, one might say, so much want to be friends with their children that they dislike the idea of authority altogether and unconsciously welcome any confusion that masks its essence. In education, certainly, as far as most liberal societies are concerned, the ideas marked by 'authority', 'obedience' and 'discipline' have more or less sunk without trace, even if the words are reinterpreted to suit contemporary fashion. ('Discipline', we read in one well-known educational textbook, 'means keeping the pupils stimulated and concerned.')

(b) The second cure consists, again very obviously, of a serious attempt to engender trust and communication. Though both cures need to be operated, it is very important to preserve a clear distinction between the two. Without that, and without seeing the point of each, we relapse into a disastrous style of thinking along a certain dimension marked perhaps by 'tough-minded' at one end of the scale and 'tender-minded' at the other. (Thus we feel that we ought to be a bit tough on criminals in prison because, after all, they are criminals; then again we feel that we ought not to be too tough because, after all, we are kind people; so we occupy a kind of muddled middle position.) It is not a matter of trying to adjust a balance, a judicious admixture of tough rule-making and enforcing and tender communication and kindness: it is a matter of operating two different and parallel enterprises. It is one thing to act as an authority, another to act as an equal. Nothing is gained, and a lot lost, by adopting any kind of half-and-half position.

Trust and communication take time to produce. Among the things that accelerate them, formal procedures and most of what goes on under the heading of 'participation' are not numbered. Moreover, any attempt has to be genuine: it is no good for middle-aged members of staff to pretend to be at home in a disco or for students to pretend that their natural habitat is at the high table — though both groups may, of course, learn to acquire the taste. Efficient methods are necessarily informal; they are also likely to be simple in content — eating and drinking together, playing games together, engaging in joint tasks that stress what is common to both parties rather than the peculiar tastes or expertise of either. A research project on how much time is in fact spent in such joint activities would be well worth undertaking; if the results were as dismal as we should anticipate, we can hardly be surprised at the persistent cold war.

It will be evident that these procedures are far removed not only from political participation but also from most of what goes on under clinical headings like 'pastoral care' and 'counselling'. Even our own phraseology — 'procedures' for 'engendering trust' — is dangerous: what is required, quite simply, is that at least some members of staff should actually like being with their students in an informal context and that the students should like it too. This involves the requirements that the institution should appoint people on that principle and should recognize the job (another dangerous term) as an essential one. It is not everybody's cup of tea: perhaps the most serious difficulty in education is how to get enough people of the right sort. The reason why we have to take it seriously, which is also the reason why it is apt to become over-stylized and clinical, is simply that this kind of informal interaction is in very short supply. The reasons for this in turn are various. Some are simple, such as shortage of time and pressure of work; others, however, are fantasy-based, one predominant fantasy being that the students do not need it and/or do not want it. Of these the first is always false and the latter usually false. Any serious or genuine education depends on a kind of parenting. The idea that young people, or indeed people of almost any age, are able and willing to engage in serious and sustained learning without a supporting background of this kind seems to us extremely simple-minded.

We have so far failed to distinguish, under this general heading, contexts of interaction that are (1) egalitarian or (2) patronizing. (Both these pieces of terminology are odious: almost any terminology is.) We mean simply that there will naturally be times when the two parties meet as equals (most obviously, for instance, when drinking, or talking, or playing some kind of game together on neutral ground) and other times when one entertains the other (as it were on home ground). Both are important for both parties, allowing everyone the opportunity to forget all about temporary or permanent differences of status on the one hand and, on the other, to patronise or be patronized. One advantage of the former is that contexts may be chosen — a suitable kind of game, for example — that permit the natural talents of youth to outshine those of the staff; in the latter case, it is perhaps particularly important that the students should be expected and encouraged to invite staff into the students' territory, which puts the students temporarily into a position of power. (One of the awful things about being educated is that people are always doing something to you, whether nice or nasty. An occasional reversal of this general role is extremely desirable.)

A somewhat more direct assault on the problem would make use of the well-tried device of mutual satire. A great deal of tension was defused or brought under control at one school in which one of us worked, where various age-groups (staff, prefects, younger pupils and so on) or working-groups (school matrons, secretaries, caretakers, etc.) put on sketches that parodied other groups. This seems a grossly naive device and one which, of course, needs very careful working out, but it provides a much better medium (both psychologically and aesthetically) than, for instance, the writing of articles in school or student magazines. The opportunity to laugh at oneself or what one stands for is not only a test of sanity but also (if taken) a generator of it. More problematic because of the dangers of clinical formality, but in our judgement worth trying if supported by other less formal contexts, is the even more direct method of holding seminars or working groups designed to encourage the necessary insight. However, much one's temperament may react against the more extravagant or (as it were)

Californian versions of encounter groups and other therapy groups, it seems feeble-minded or intellectually dishonest not to make some such attempt. The alternative is simply to allow each side to go on thinking dark thoughts (and some of them are unbelievably dark) about the other but never to have these expressed in any joint context — or, rather, to let them surface only when written up on the banners of demonstrators or chanted by them. In general, the more intellectually sophisticated the institution (Oxbridge is a fair example), the stronger the mental defences against attempting any such thing: we preserve the pretence that all or most of us, students as well as staff, are too level-headed or sensible to require such treatment or, alternatively, that it is not our business ('We are a university, not a mental hospital'). Anyone who does not perceive the element of fantasy here is unlikely to be persuaded by anything that we write.

The Future

There is, of course, much more to be written about this (particularly, perhaps, in connection with trust and communication) at all levels of discourse and with the aid of many disciplines. But we are inclined to believe that not much will be gained unless the matter is taken seriously in the right sort of way, a way that, as far as we can see, involves academic or intellectual sophistication less than personal honesty — to put it brutally, the willingness to own up. We do not expect it will help people to do this if we add that we have not only made precisely the mistakes we have been criticizing in the past but also continue to make them in the present, but it would be dishonest of us not to admit that the major mistake — a sort of second-order or methodological error — in our own experience is the temptation to look away from what are fairly obvious facts under the pretence of intellectual disagreement.

Be that as it may: we want finally to suggest some reasons why the future may give grounds for pessimism — other things being equal: of course, a new sustaining and universal ideology may arise, solving our problems if only temporarily — and why, in consequence, very stern efforts will have to be made by educators (not much is to be hoped for from politicians). First, such consensus as exists in our own and most liberal societies is diminishing rather than increasing. Secondly, there is on the whole a lessening trust in educators: education is increasingly politicized and subject to more and more external pressure. It is characteristic of liberal societies not to trust people with power; unfortunately, quite a lot of power and autonomy is required for effective education. Thirdly, the fashion for integration and mass homogeneous education is likely to continue, making it increasingly difficult to decentralize institutions in a way that enables them to generate and enforce clear contracts. Last, the continued existence of anything above a minimum level of education is, of course, dependent on a tolerably well ordered and well-off society, and it is at least possible that our own society will become worse in both respects, as a result chiefly of our failure to understand and to put into operation precisely those truths that we have been describing in the limited context of staff—student conflicts.

Undeterred by ending on such a dramatic note, one might also express an equally futuristic hope: that at least some educational institutions will be able to survive this sort of future. If they do, it will not only be because they are able to remain economically viable over what may be a long period of shortage and politically viable over what may be a long period of chaos, but also because they have a firm grasp of the relevant concepts. It is to be hoped, though the hope may (for obvious psychological reasons) be a tenuous one, that this grasp will not be enshrined in or distorted by any particular ideological straitjacket — though even that, perhaps, would be significantly better than nothing (one is grateful to the monasteries for keeping education alive after Rome fell, whatever one may think of the Christian religion). Thoughts of this kind may naturally be written off as a kind of fantasy; pictures of the world, or a certain kind of world, coming to an end are clinically recognizable and explainable. Nevertheless, it is also possible to see the standard reaction of believing in a sufficiently solid residue of 'common sense', perhaps almost a British orthodoxy, as in its own way equally delusory. Naturally, fashions (such as some of the student unrest in the 1960s) come and go, and it is just possible to argue that students may become incapable of the rationality required for effective corporate action as quickly as the staff of educational institutions may become incapable of it, and for much the same reasons: the world changes too quickly; they become disenchanted with the minimal results; and there is a constant temptation to abandon collective causes and to retreat into the inner confines of the self; adding, perhaps, some salvationist religion or some other vigilantly guarded sanctum to make a life of 'doing one's own thing' tolerable. But that is hardly cause for complacency.

10

The Empirical Disciplines and Educational Research

By 'empirical disciplines' we refer not only to psychology and sociology in their various forms, but also to other candidates for relevance to education — anthropology, clinical psychotherapy, even perhaps literary criticism. In what sense some or all of these are 'empirical disciplines' is an open and important question, about which we shall say something later: for the present we shall take it that 'empirical' is to do with matters of fact, which (granted that 'fact' is a slippery term) may be roughly contrasted with matters of value on the one hand and matters of meaning or logic on the other. By 'education' we refer to a practical enterprise, broadly definable as the intentional generation of sustained and serious learning (see chapter 2). That too can be questioned, but not with any relevance to what follows.

Since education is a practical enterprise, any part or programme of education will aim at some good: the better learning of French, or improved 'pastoral care', or whatever. Deciding on the good to be aimed at is clearly not primarily an empirical matter, though empirical facts might show it to be practically impossible to achieve (for lack of resources or talent, for example); it is subject to whatever rational procedures we take to apply to questions of value. Nobody seriously believes that there are no such procedures: not only all discussion of education but the enterprise itself assumes that we can make more or less rational judgements in this matter. Equally, defining the good more clearly (what is to count as

'French' or 'pastoral care', or what we are to mean by these terms)
is not an empirical inquiry. For both tasks logic and conceptual
clarity are plainly important, in the way we have described earlier
(see chapter 5).

Hence the natural and sensible way to conduct any educational
research would be, very obviously, first to define clearly the good
aimed at and then to determine by means of the empirical
disciplines how that good may most easily be achieved (though
there is an important over-simplification here, since the achievement of some objectives logically — not just empirically or as a
matter of fact — requires certain methods. To use a partial analogy,
we first determine where we want to go and then find out from
geographers or explorers or other relevant parties how best to get
there. That is, in fact, how many maps first came to be made:
traders or missionaries or other people with specific practical
objectives collected facts related to those objectives. The idea of
simply 'making a map', without this kind of objective, is a much
later development. Indeed — and this is one reason why the
empirical disciplines can never be entirely unrelated to human
goods or objectives — the idea of a map divorced from a purpose
is an incoherent idea, since maps must always be made from a
certain point of view — for use by the sailor, or the motorist, or the
hiker, or whoever. Maps show some things and not other things;
they could not, logically, show everything, since even what counts
as a thing to be shown will depend on some specific human
interest.

As the immense variety of approaches adopted in psychology
and the social sciences abundantly shows, our interests in mapping
the 'facts' about human beings may be very different. Experimental
psychologists take one cross-section, ethnomethodologists another,
literary critics and fiction writers a third. But from the educator's
viewpoint, all these approaches are severely limited by the fact
that they are not geared to any practical (let alone any educational)
good. In that sense they are 'academic'. The educator wishes (or
should wish, since many educators seem to have lost their nerve or
their common sense in this respect) to make a journey from A to
B: the academic disciplines give him information analogous to that
which might be given to a traveller by, say, someone who was only
interested in rock strata, or botany, or wild life. What such a
person had to offer could not be dismissed (precipices, yams and

tigers are not irrelevant to the traveller), but the information would nonetheless be severely limited.

The other defect of these approaches is not a limitation but a distortion. Just because each approach is based on a certain interest, it inevitably forces on anyone who adopts it (for whatever purpose) a certain viewpoint, a prescription about what is to count as the 'facts'. Thus, looking at hooliganism on football terraces, an ethnomethodologist will see different individuals playing particular roles in a complex drama, a sociologist perhaps some kind of protest by working-class youths against a culture that oppresses them and so on. By contrast, a moralist will describe the 'facts' in terms of anti-social or immoral behaviour, a religious believer in terms of the breaking of God's commandments or of a failure in Christian harmony. The educator's interest is different again: he will be concerned with some change in the hooligans' behaviour brought about by *learning* (not just by any procedure — education is different from propaganda or other forms of social change). In so far as the educator adopts approaches dictated by other (non-educational) interests, he is like the traveller who is tacitly persuaded by this or that approach to view the terrain in particular terms, to see his journey as a movement from one type of rock stratum to another, or from poor to rich civilizations, or as a religious pilgrimage.

There is one respect particularly in which this limitation and distortion, inherent in any empirical discipline (and therefore not a failing of the discipline as such), is likely to be disastrous for the educator. For it is not just that the educator undertakes a practical journey with a practical aim: it is also that he undertakes a journey of a particular kind. The educator is concerned with learning, and learning is something that people do, not something which happens to them. In this respect education is unlike, say, medicine or economics. Health and a plentiful supply of food are both things that, in general, people can be simply given, as they can be given cleaner air or more money; but the benefits of learning they must gain for themselves, with however much or little help and encouragement. The virtues of a good learner are, in a broad sense, moral — or, as people sometimes say nowadays, 'psychological' — virtues: enthusiasm, determination, accuracy, conscientiousness, imagination and so forth. Learning also involves the conscious deployment of rationality, attention to rules, standards and criteria of success, the sustained intention of making progress. It is a paradigmatic case of human endeavour. Now, the empirical disciplines, for the most part, view human beings 'scientifically' — that is, as patients rather than as agents. Unsurprisingly, they tend to see people as 'products' of society or 'cases' resulting from bad child-rearing, or to regard them as 'playing roles' inherent in a particular form of social interaction. In particular, the concept of *moral blame* will not be applied.

This is disastrous for education because it creates the impression that children and other students are not learners but recipients. Nothing is their fault (or their merit either). Education forgets its essential nature and becomes a matter of simply doing things to children, or for them, or against them — anyway they are on the receiving end. The empirical disciplines are apt to take education away from its natural home, which it shares with other enterprises that also stress the human being as agent — non-directive psychotherapy, the work of the priest and the parent and (if this too has not become corrupted) social work. It is precisely the refusal of these disciplines to have anything to do with 'values' — particularly moral values, which very few people are bold enough to tangle with nowadays in liberal societies — that makes them force educators to wear spectacles that distort their vision of their own enterprises: in effect, very dark glasses that render obscure what is essential to it.

We do not, of course, want to argue that nothing valuable may be learned from the empirical disciplines. Some, as we hinted earlier, are improperly so called because they are in a sense also practical enterprises with objectives and goods of their own. Literature and psychotherapy (and we would add philosophy) aim, in their various ways, at clarifying and purging the heart and mind, at increasing rationality, ego-strength and imagination. These objectives are either themselves educational (since they involve learning) or sufficiently like those of education to render them of great value to the educator. But the supposedly 'scientific' disciplines have to date offered us little that is obviously relevant and helpful: if practical education is any better today than it was fifty years ago (a doubtful assumption), it is not because we have made giant strides in educational research based on psychology and social science. And the basic cause is not that there are fundamental difficulties and misconceptions about the whole methodology of social science (though that is also true) but rather that the work of those who direct these disciplines has been almost totally disconnected from educational objectives, even if (which is not commonly the case) those objectives have been shown to be desirable and have been made fully and unambiguously clear.

In suggesting a new kind of relationship between the empirical disciplines and education, we may find it helpful to return to our analogy. What the traveller wants is not just any information but information about whatever may make his journey from A to B difficult or easy, in particular (since where it is easy he has no problems) information about the nature of the opposition, as we may call it. He must, of course, have a clear objective, and a clearly desirable one, in the first place, otherwise the information will be irrelevant, and he will quite rightly be told (though not by the empirical disciplines) either that he has not specified the place he wants to get to clearly enough or that it is not a desirable place to go to. He must also show that his (specifically educational) journey is necessary — that it is necessary that he, an educator, gets to B rather than that somebody else (a propagandist or some other non-rational agent of social change) should make the journey instead. Given all that, he can then demand information that will help him.

The example of football hooliganism will serve us here. Non-educational objectives could be gained by, say, simply banning certain people from the football grounds, or not playing the matches, or making all the spectators sit in straightjackets. The educator wants the hooligans to *learn* something: presumably, to appreciate, and act on the appreciation, that certain rules of behaviour are desirable. He would not have much trouble in showing that there were such desirable rules or in specifying what they were clearly; what he wants is an answer to the question 'How can these people be taught to keep the rules?' or 'What kinds of pressure or influence can we bring to bear that will make such a person say (and act on the saying) "I had better keep the rules"?' Now, these questions are not enormously hard to answer. Not much research (and practically no research along the orthodox lines of social science) would be required to show that we needed (1) a clear and well publicized statement about what the rules of behaviour were, (2) sufficient explanation, particularly to potential offenders, about why they were necessary and (3) a set of sanctions, of whatever form and in whatever strength turned out to be adequate, that would ensure that the rules were kept. It would help to have (4) a full account of the types of temptation likely to operate against keeping the rules and, no doubt, (5) some general account of how young people learned to keep rules of that type. But on the whole the case seems to be a comparatively simple one, requiring chiefly clarity about our objectives and common sense in pursuing them.

Yet the fact is that despite universal condemnation of football hooliganism and some very sophisticated research about what goes on in the stands and terraces, such clarity and common sense seem to be lacking. A lady whose arm had been broken at a football match put the point clearly: 'What they want to do research on is why the authorities don't stop it.' It is quite clear, whether or not this particular example is acceptable, that a great deal of failure in educational practice is not only moral or 'psychological' failure but moral or 'psychological' failure *on the part of the authorities.* It is not, or certainly not always, that we need more general 'scientific' information about human beings, nor even that we need more information about them in relation to specifically educational objectives. It is rather that we need more information about why we will not, or cannot, or at any rate do not formulate clear and clearly desirable objectives and pursue them even in those (many) cases in which only common sense is required to show us how.

There is nothing very surprising in this as long as we remember what sort of enterprise education is. It is entirely clear that one of the most important — almost certainly the most important — feature of any educational situation consists of the presence or absence of certain moral (again, in a broad sense) qualities in the educational authorities themselves: not just the teacher but also the head teacher, the local authorities, the advisers, the governments and, indeed, the educational researcher. In just the same way it is the moral qualities of the parent, the priest and the psychotherapist that really count as much as, or more than, research into their clients. On any account, such jobs involve a good deal of autonomy if they are to be done properly, and only increasing the nerve, conceptual clarity, confidence, awareness and imagination of those who do the jobs is likely to improve their performance. It is not, or not only, a matter of giving clear-headed, secure and psychologically impeccable travellers some 'facts' or 'methods' that will help them on their journey: it is more a matter of improving the travellers' own morale and moral qualities.

Recently the stringent and behaviouristic application of social science to educational problems without bothering much about teachers has fallen somewhat out of favour, and rightly; but it has been (partly) replaced by something no better — deference to teachers or other educational authorities, who are now supposed to identify the problems and to set the objectives, calling on workers in the empirical disciplines to perform the humble task of telling them (or suggesting to them) how to get what they want. The absurdity of this deference — a part of that general deference to 'consensus' or to the consumer that marks a society that no longer accepts established or traditional values but can think of nothing better than to follow fashions and climates of opinions — lies in its refusal to face the fact that the authorities do not always have the qualities they should have. It is of no use to react to this by mere lamentation: we urgently need research into why they do not always have such qualities (or display them, for they may have them but lack the nerve to use them). We need to know what exactly is going wrong in this case or that, just where, and for what reasons, teachers and others lose their nerve, or are made to feel insecure, or are muddled, or over-influenced by fashion and fantasy, or lack the powers to do what they know quite well to be sensible.

In a word, we are saying that the central relationship between the empirical disciplines and education should operate via the educators as much as (and, we think, much more than) those being educated. A little work has, of course, been done in this area (on teacher perception, for instance), but it has been grossly over-influenced by the particular interests of researchers in the grip of more general sociological or psychological (rather than educational) interests. If teachers do not have a clear grasp of what is or should be marked by 'discipline', 'moral education', 'learning French', 'pastoral care' and many other terms, and/or if they do not hold the relevant concepts steadily enough in their minds to see what methods are required by common sense and what need further research, and/or if they succeed in all this but are inhibited by the law, or the examination system, or other conditions of their work, how can we hope for serious progress? And how can we remedy any of these failures without getting much clearer than we now are about when and why they occur?

Many educational researchers, perhaps particularly among the younger generation, might accept the substance of what we have said but find themselves up against an ingrained tradition of deference to certain established practices in educational research. We need to understand what lies behind this tradition. Elsewhere one of us has tried, in some detail, to identify some features in educational research that are, fairly obviously, intellectually misguided (Wilson, 1972). Behind these and other similar features, however, lie certain more basic attitudes and approaches too general and too deep-rooted to be described as 'methodological'. We are inclined to believe that unless and until researchers (and those engaged in controlling and funding research) become conscious of these attitudes and reject them with understanding, the more intellectually disreputable features of educational research are likely to be glossed over. In other words, we are dealing with an area in which improvement will come as much from insight and emotional honesty as from the application of logic.

One of the more obvious symptoms of the current malaise is the pseudo-scholarship of much educational writing. Researchers — particularly if they are engaged in writing scholarly dissertations — often feel, and are often told by their supervisors and advisers, that they must 'cover the ground' or 'take account of the literature'. That advice is, of course, harmless as it stands, but it immediately raises the question of what ground is worth covering and what literature is authoritative or at least useful. Here almost everything turns on what one thinks about the general state of education as a subject of scholarly inquiry. If one believes — and a very large number of people do (rightly) believe this, although they do not always find it politic to say so — that many educational problems are in much the same state as scientific or medical problems were in the Middle Ages, then the whole idea of there being a large and respectable body of literature in the background has been dropped. There is no such body, and we are all beginners.

Whether or not existing practice (or theory) is worth looking at in any detail, then, depends on how sensible and intellectually reputable it is likely to be. It would be a bold (or a very ignorant) researcher, we think, who believed that there were many areas of educational inquiry in which there was anything like solid and definitive knowledge that could be built on, as (today, but less so in A D 1200) we can build on work in the natural sciences. There are, of course, some. If we are concerned with non-disputable facts of some kind — the numbers of children attending certain schools, the cost of school meals, correlations between parental income group and passes in examinations — then we are tolerably safe, but as soon as we venture (as we can hardly avoid venturing) on more strictly educational ground, we find ourselves in a quagmire of fashion and ideology. Partly for this reason, many researchers undertake research into some purely sociological or at any rate (as they hope) factual area. For instance, we know of one researcher into 'moral education' who has spent a great many years simply reporting and describing (in neutral terms, he imagines, and without 'value judgements') what various past and present cultures say and do under that heading. He has covered a lot of interesting ground in telling us how they socialize their children in Korea, the Seychelles, San Diego, Balham and many other places, and what the prevailing opinions about moral education are or were among parents in fifteenth-century France, twentieth-century Greece and Nazi Germany in the 1940s. All this is great fun, much as the analyses of football hooliganism and other phenomena by contemporary ethnomethodologists are great fun. But it does not, of course, tell us anything about how we or anyone else ought to educate our children in morality, any more than analyses of football hooliganism tell us how people ought to behave during football matches and how to educate them so that they do so behave.

Our fear of making 'value judgements' is just the tip of an iceberg. It is as if, to sustain this somewhat dramatic metaphor, there were a vast frozen and non-negotiable area between observation of what goes on and the taking of some sensible and decisive action. Continuous and addictive sociology and psychology seep into the area. We go on observing and trying to explain instead of setting up some demonstrably desirable objective and thinking in practical terms about how to achieve it. Once we have a tolerably clear idea of what moral education ought to look like or what sort of behaviour we want at football grounds, it will be largely a waste of time to pursue lengthy inquiries into what happens in Indonesian moral education or Patagonian football. We need anyway to begin by establishing clear objectives, for otherwise we shall not know just what existing practices to place under the microscope. To take an example from one fashionable area, 'community education': we need to have a clear idea of what is to count as 'community education' to start with and what ends it is supposed to serve. This is by no means easy, but without it we shall not know whether to include (for instance) Israeli *kibbutzim,* Hitler Youth Camps, Christadelphians, village schools, the IRA, monasteries or the Oxford college system. What 'ground' shall we 'cover'? What 'literature' shall we 'take stock of'? Without some clear idea the chances are that we shall do no more than read the more fashionable books that have the words 'community education' in their titles, from which we may then 'collect definitions' of community education in an endeavour to 'define our terms'. This last is, for the professional philosopher, at once the saddest and the clearest case of irrational deference: it is as if researchers believed that the right way to get clear is to accept what various writers in the past — usually with muddled heads and plenty of axes to grind — have propounded as 'definitions'.

Genuine research, as we know quite well when we keep our heads, does not proceed like this. The scientists who first gave us solid knowledge about the physical world did not spend most of their time in 'covering the ground', which was then littered with astrologers and seekers after the *elixir vitae,* and the men who gave us vaccination and penicillin did not conduct surveys of old wives and witchdoctors. They succeeded because they were wedded to the right method of research, a method that was sharply opposed to prevailing and past practice. They had nerve, clear heads and a strong desire to get at the truth. When this (scientific) method was established, they read and listened to other people who were also wedded to it. The main hope for the future of educational research is that a sufficiently large number of people will emerge who have the courage, as well as the ability, to use the empirical disciplines in the way that education itself requires.

Select Bibliography

Barrow, R. (1981) *The Philosophy of Schooling* (London: Wheatsheaf)

Dearden, R. F. (1968) *Philosophy of Primary Education* (London: Routledge & Kegan Paul)

Dearden, R. F. *et al.* (eds.) (1972) *Education and the Development of Reason* (London: Routledge & Kegan Paul)

Flew, A. (1976) *Sociology, Equality and Education* (London: Macmillan)

Hannan, C. *et al.* (eds.) (1976) *The First Year of Teaching* (Harmondsworth: Penguin)

Highet, G. (1951) *The Art of Teaching* (London: Methuen)

Hirst, P. H., and Peters, R. S. (1970) *The Logic of Education* (London: Routledge & Kegan Paul)

Loukes, H. (1959) *The Castle and the Field* (London: Allen & Unwin)

Loukes, H. (1961) *Teenage Religion* (London: SCM Press)

Loukes, H. (1965) *New Ground in Christian Education* (London: SCM Press)

Loukes, H. (1973) *Teenage Morality* (London: SCM Press)

Norwood, C. (1929) *The English Tradition of Education* (London: John Murray)

Peters, R. S. (1959) *Authority, Responsibility and Education* (London: Allen & Unwin)

Peters, R. S. (1966) *Ethics and Education* (London: Allen & Unwin)

Tibble, J. W. (ed.) (1966) *The Study of Education* (London: Routledge & Kegan Paul)

Warnock, G. (1971) *The Object of Morality* (London: Methuen)

Warnock, M. (1977) *Schools of Thought* (London: Faber & Faber)

Wilson, J. (1972) *Philosophy and Educational Research* (Slough: National Foundation of Educational Research)

Wilson, J. (1973) *A Teacher's Guide to Moral Education* (London: Chapman)

Wilson, J. (1975) *Educational Theory and the Preparation of Teachers* (Slough: National Foundation of Educational Research)

Wilson, J. (1977) *Philosophy and Practical Education* (London: Routledge & Kegan Paul)

Wilson, J. (1979a) *Fantasy and Common Sense in Education* (Oxford: Martin Robertson)

Wilson, J. (1979b) *Preface to the Philosophy of Education* (London: Routledge & Kegan Paul)

Wilson, J. (1980) *Love, Sex and Feminism* (New York: Praeger)

Wilson, J. (1981) *Discipline and Moral Education* (Slough: NFER—Nelson)

Index